BREACH

HOW THE
NEXT GENERATION
ARE CONSCIOUSLY
DISRUPTING THE WORLD

Scan here to shop
for Award winning,
Sustainable,
Organic, freshly
made Skin care and
make up

BREACH

HOW THE NEXT GENERATION ARE CONSCIOUSLY DISRUPTING THE WORLD

RONEN AIRES

Published and distributed by Merack Publishing

Library of Congress Control Number: 2021917797
Aires, Ronen
BREACH: How the Next Generation are Consciously Disrupting the World

ISBN:
Paperback 978-1-949635-72-0
Hardcover 978-1-949635-74-4
eBook 978-1-949635-73-7

Dedicated to Kimmy.

My girls: Kiki, Dani, Gabsi
and their entire generation

You are doing amazing things.

CONTENTS

Let's be honest
Our world is a mess
Like an aging human body after decades of neglect
Our world is in a state of disease
Can it re-calibrate to heal itself?

Let's be honest
Without any radical change, our future looks bleak
But there is a new force in our world
And it's shaping our future

Think of it as a single, connected, decentralized organism
That may just be the answer we've been looking for
With new thoughts, beliefs and habits
It holds the key to our future

This force is everywhere among us
And its sole purpose is to fix
the broken world it was born into

This force is made up of builders and destroyers
Some lead with their heart
Some lead with contempt
Their joint mission is tearing down the status quo which got
us into this mess in the first place

Their collective efforts are gaining momentum
Causing unbearable pressure
And something is about to blow
Prepare for BREACH… lots of them!

Each breach may be ugly
Definitely inconvenient
And nothing will be spared
In order to birth a new world

A world in which we live in harmony with each other and
with nature
A world of shared humanity - oneness
Let's be honest
The alternative is Armageddon

My wish is that the younger generation realizes their
potential to usher in a new world
One that we all want to live in
*One that, "we cannot see from here but can commit to shaping,
regardless"[1]*
We should all live with radical hope for a better future

---

1   "Radical Hope: Ethics in the Face of Cultural Devastation."
(Lear, Jonathan, Cambridge, Mass: Harvard University Press), 2006.

SECTION 1
THE INTRODUCTION

CHAPTER ONE
THE YOUNG ELDER

When people ask what I do, I don't know how to answer the question. You would think I'd have an answer prepared, as this question arises at every party, get together, networking event, and whenever you meet someone new. In today's society, "What do you do?" is as common as "What is your name?" and "How are you?" It's at the top of the list when you are getting to know someone. I've tried to come up with a canned description of what I do, a simple cookie-cutter term that doesn't require copious amounts of further explanation—but nothing fits. What do I do? Well, it depends.

I am a disruptor of stereotypical beliefs. I am a thinker, opening people's minds to different perspectives. I am an agent of change—uplifting, inspiring and igniting a spark in others to take action. I am a connector, building a bridge between generations. I am an advocate, a listener, a facilitator, a guide. How do you explain all of that in five words or less?

The best I can come up with is this: I am an Elder. A Young Elder—for, at forty-five years young at the time I write this book, I understand that I still have a lot of learning to do. In my role as Young Elder, I am a go between—a connection between the past and the future. With one foot in the past, I listen and learn from the wisdom of those who have come before me. With one foot in the future, I listen and learn from the village youth, who are carving their own path. An Elder's primary role is to use his or her wisdom and experience to guide and advise the village youth, yet I feel as though I learn as much from them as they do from me.

My role as a Young Elder is not one-sided. I am not the one who holds and bestows all knowledge. Instead, I consider myself to be a gatherer of knowledge, looking to those who came before and those who came after me. I believe we are all in this life together, and sharing our experiences allows us all to rise up. I admire, and am infinitely inspired, by youth. Their creativity and big ideas give me hope. There is strength in their naivety. There is value in looking through the world through the lens of innocence. This view should not be brushed aside as silly or inexperienced. I look toward those in the older generations for wisdom. They have gained decades of experience through trial and error. They can navigate delicate situations with tact and restraint. This insight matters and should not be brushed aside as antiquated or prehistoric. In order to make sustainable change in this world, we need both sides of the equation— young and old—working together toward a common goal, whether that's a kinder version of capitalism, work-life integration, political change or social justice.

And so, I am the bridge. I am the guy who connects the old and the young, and helps them make progress. I am the guy who will encourage both sides to put aside their stereotypical beliefs—their "Us versus Them" mentality—and illuminate the inherent value each can offer. If we can take the wisdom and experience gathered by the establishment, and apply the lens of youthful fresh eyes, the world would be a very different place. A better place.

I strongly believe our youth will change this world. They are exploding with idealism, curiosity, passion, and innovation. The youngest generations hold the key to change because they are not afraid to be radical. They disregard the rules of politics as if they have an allergy to the status quo. They are not constrained by antiquated ideas about the ways things "should" be done. They are only limited by their own drive and imagination—both of which seem to be endless.

> Our youth will change this world

I have spent my entire adult life crafting this vision and attempting to make it a reality. One might call me a "youth-tivist"—a passionate advocate for the younger generations. It seems to be a rite of passage, this cycle of graduation: younger people coming up to disrupt and oppose the values of those who came before them. I advocate for the disruption. I cheer it on—encourage it, even. Each generation has a purpose, you see. Part of that purpose is to question the status quo and create change. While this may appear to be disrespectful to those who came before them, it is a necessary proponent of growth and evolution.

Elders are wise enough to expect a certain amount of change, but we like it incrementally. We prefer change to be delivered in small, palatable doses so as to maintain a certain level of comfort and predictability. This generation of youth has not adopted the bite-sized mentality. They don't want to navigate the system that was created for them, and work patiently to create methodical long-term change. After looking at the systems in which they are expected to navigate, they hit the unsubscribe button and proceeded to blow things up.

Effective disruption requires a forum to organize and communicate. While it was not my original intention, I may have created such a space. One of my greatest professional accomplishments has been the creation of Student Village.

In the year 2000, we lived in a pre-Google, pre-Facebook, and pre-Twitter era. At that time, I was a recent college graduate from the University of Witwatersrand (WITS) in Johannesburg, South Africa. As expected, I found a job and tried to live the corporate life I was brought up to revere. While it was exciting for a short while, after three years, I found myself questioning my purpose. I was having an existential crisis at the ripe old age of twenty-five. Why wait until mid-life to have a crisis? No mid-life crisis for me. Why wait that long to begin questioning everything about my life? Instead, I raced right toward a quarter-life meltdown. Such an overachiever!

All jokes aside, I knew in my heart that I was destined to make a massive difference in the world, so I began to look at the world around me, wondering where I would make my mark.

It seemed many of my friends were struggling to adjust to life after studenthood. While they were surrounded by job opportunities, they complained that because of their young age and inexperience, no one would take them seriously. Making matters worse, many of my peers lacked sound career advice, interview skills, even budgeting capabilities. There was simply no forum for connection among young adults, no community for students like us who were transitioning into the next phase of life. My friends and I spent hours lamenting the vast disconnect between what we *thought* life would be like and what it *actually* turned out to be. We didn't like the roles we were expected to play. Life felt unfulfilling and meaningless.

It was then that I heard my calling. After countless late nights dreaming and scheming with a couple of friends, I decided to quit my corporate job. Along with two like-minded friends—Jason Glick and Marc Kornberger—we started a website for college students. In reflecting on our own college experience, Jason and I often reminisce about the good times but also lament about the challenges of being young and misunderstood. ***Students are not taken seriously. Their unique perspectives and innovative ways are often ignored, discounted or written off.*** We felt that youth should have a voice and should be provided with access to opportunities. As a collective, they have value.

Funded by advertising, this small project quickly morphed into something bigger. It seemed that youth craved opportunities to discuss student issues, job opportunities, life skill development and more. Student Village became a large-scale launch pad, connecting brands to youth and vice versa. We helped give youth a voice by facilitating inspired, authentic, and engaging connections between brands and youth. Many brands and tens of thousands of careers have been launched through Student Village over the past twenty years.

It is from that viewpoint that I write this book. Observing, learning from, and serving our youth has become my life's work. The younger generations, while naïve, are not to be discounted. They are a key driving force for sustainable change. My intent in writing this is to show you their value, to introduce you to their innovative way of thinking. Different is not wrong, it is simply unfamiliar and deserves a chance. As elders, we need to listen to the youth and learn to understand them.

Their naivety doesn't derive from a lack of knowledge or a lack of global awareness. In this respect they are quite informed, or "woke" as the kids say. Their awareness has inspired lofty goals and strong morals, creative ideas and a deconstruction of the status quo. My use of the word "naivety" refers to their lack of experience. They are young and they may not yet have the skills necessary to execute their divine vision for a more inclusive, innovative world. That's where the elders come in. Rather than attempting to force young people to conform— squeezing them into the confines of expectations we grew up with—we need to validate their dreams and nurture the skills they need to achieve them like creative problem solving, collaboration and critical thinking. We have the ability to fast-track their success.

If you are a business owner, it should be recognized that today's youth make up your current and future consumers. In fact, Generation Z, also known as centennials (those born between the years 1996-2010), make up the largest consumer population in the United States—an estimated 27% of the total population and hold enormous spending power.[2] Companies need to take youth seriously because they either are or will become a future customer or future leader. We need to harness their power and grow *with it* instead of fighting against it.

Youth have come into this world with different "factory settings." While we are all living and breathing humans, youth are an upgraded version of those before them. They live in a digital world and this is the direction in which companies need to change. If you don't want to be relegated as a dinosaur— if you want your business to stay relevant—you need to authentically understand and care about youth.

As the Young Elder of the village, I suggest you read this book with an open mind, an open heart and an eye toward the future. I won't deny, the next generations of youth are

---

2   "Generation Z News Latest Characteristics, Research, And Facts," (Business Insider, 2021), https://www.businessinsider.com/generation-z?r=AU&IR=T.

certainly making uncomfortable changes. They are breaching the traditional ways of thinking, pushing against the status quo with incredible force. They are open to collaboration with those who have come before them, hoping we honor their ideals and support their movements. They need us to guide them so the change they make is powerful and sustainable. They cannot do it alone, although they are not afraid to try!

While youth are asking for support, they are not willing to engage in a wrestling match for control. Their belief in change is so confident that they are willing to destroy the establishment in order to re-create it. Elders need to accept that change is happening with or without us and now is the time for us to choose. We can either support those who are fighting to make our world a better, more equitable place or we can resist because change is scary and uncomfortable.

Without our support this generation will continue to move forward and alter the world as we know it, but I prefer to imagine the realm of possibilities they could achieve if we stood with them, offering guidance and support.

Youth need you, and whether or not you know it yet, you need them too.

CHAPTER TWO
BREACH

I was raised to be compliant, not to question authority. My own factory setting was that of "silent rebel." While, outwardly, I did as I was told, inwardly I questioned everything around me—my parents, my grandparents, my teachers, my family's business. I was a reluctant team player, towing the line to do what was needed and expected.

The "because I said so" culture I was raised in became deeply ingrained in me. The other phrase commonly heard in my household was, "If I don't do it myself, it won't be done properly." Ironically, as an adult these phrases became the mentality with which I led my company—using my years of accumulated knowledge and experience to forge the professional path. I hired the best and the brightest, grooming them to be successful in bringing my dream to fruition, frantically micromanaging their every move. The caveat was I work with youth, and they didn't seem to share my vision or respond to my leadership style—control freak. They didn't buy into the hierarchy and didn't want to be controlled.

This is one of the complexities of my personality—my inner rebel fighting to become untangled from the conformity I grew up with. It has taken years to unravel myself from this web and separate myself from my childhood. I recognize the need to trust others, but find it easier said than done.

I think of myself as open-minded. One of my core strengths is my ability and willingness to understand youth—to see them the way they desire to be seen and to meet them where they are at. I have always worked to find a common ground from which we can collaborate. Despite perceiving myself as a fair and positive leader, I have felt a gradual shift in the past few years, an increasing imbalance of power swinging from my authority to their disregard for it. It's been frustrating and I'm exhausted.

When I set out to write this book, my intention was to investigate the impact of leadership style and willingness to embrace authenticity as it relates to fostering positive, collaborative working environments. I viewed myself as a translator of sorts, sharing youthful exuberance and desire with those who lead and mentor them. However, somewhere in the middle of the book, when I was eyeball deep in research, I had a profound realization. The frustration I had been feeling as a leader was not a result of my leadership style, but was due to the fact that I was expecting my employees to conform to my expectations and rise up to meet the potential I saw in them. News flash—they don't want to conform. They want to take my expectations and throw them in the garbage! It's not *they* who need to conform, it's me. In fact, it might be me who ends up in the garbage if I don't change!

I am a product of my upbringing and mentoring, just as you are. The way I was taught to lead worked perfectly fine, in my opinion. We all need to pay our dues and to learn from those who came before us. However, just because something has worked relatively well in the past, does not mean it's what is needed in this moment. And, if we truly think about it, did the hierarchy ever really work to begin with?

Perhaps I am ready to throw this system in the garbage as well.

I'm reminded of a John Mayer song:

> *Now we see everything that's going wrong*
> *With the world and those who lead it*
> *We just feel like we don't have the means*
> *To rise above and beat it*
> *So we keep waiting*
> *Waiting on the world to change*

In this book, we will spend a lot of time discussing the millennials. This generation were among the first to sense the need for drastic change. They had the right factory settings for a digital world and they called out the need to re-prioritize our lives. They didn't want to spend their days working for "the man." They desired balance and flexibility. The problem was, while the millennials may have had the vision, they didn't have the drive, so they were labeled as a generation of whiny, entitled adult-sized children. They were *waiting* for the world to change, but they didn't want to do the work.

I first envisioned this book with a different title: *They Were Right*. It still holds. I believe, if we can set ego aside and truly listen, there is a lot to be learned from the millennial generation. As this book unfolded and I journeyed right along with it, the world was also unraveling.

Usher in Generation Z. These youth have it all and that's why they fascinate me. They have the vision, the smarts and the motivation. They are the movers and the shakers and it's mystifying to some of us.

And the song still holds true:

> *Me and my friends*
> *We're all misunderstood*
> *They say we stand for nothing and*
> *There's no way we ever could*

2020 was a perfect storm of extreme global events which made drastic change not only possible, but necessary, for survival. The year began with the onset of Covid-19, a pandemic that not only dramatically altered our lives, but left bodies in its wake. This deadly virus seemed to speed up the rate of change. Schools closed, people hunkered down and the world came to a stand still. Companies had to pivot quickly in order to restructure and reimagine what was possible, simply to stay alive. Covid-19 accelerated the due course a business was headed for. If, prior to Covid-19, your business was struggling, it was now nose-diving toward a quick and painful death. If your business was flexible, adaptable and growing, this success was accelerated as well. Out of necessity, desperation and boredom, people shopped online in record numbers and many businesses thrived as a result.

2020 was the year of extremes—extreme wildfires raged across Australia. The political climate in the United States was a powder keg waiting to explode. There were massive and violent election protests. Social movements such as Black Lives Matter brought millions of people to the streets. Women all across the world, who had just begun emerging in prominent and powerful roles, suffered professionally as the need to care for their families during a global pandemic took priority.

Then, to everyone's shock and surprise, the stock market was intentionally manipulated. This event was one of the first breaches we saw, the first of many more to come. It's extremely noteworthy because, while giant hedge fund managers have been driving stock prices up and down for decades, Gamestop was the first time that small investors banded together to assert their collective will. Thousands of people used the power of their numbers to give the big guys a proper bruise. They weren't doing it for altruistic reasons. They were destroyers, wanting to cause some damage, send a message and make some money in the process.

It may come as a surprise to some of us that all of these changes were either organized, or supported, by youth, and not just a handful of progressives. There were millions of young people using their collective voice to re-establish values and systems, asserting their opinions with confidence and force. The establishment was being attacked from every possible angle: race, sex, politics, finances. It was reminiscent of David and Goliath.

I suppose you are wondering why I chose the title *Breach*.

Breach:
Noun: an act of breaking or failing to observe a law, agreement or code of conduct

This rings true. It seems that the youth have come with an operating system that has different factory settings than those who are attempting to lead them. They simply don't subscribe to our values and refuse to conform to our way of moving through this world—for better or worse. They don't play by our rules.

Breach:
Verb: to make a gap in something and break through; to rise and break through the surface of the water

Picture a volcano. It never erupts without warning. If it seems that way, it's because we have missed the subtle signs, the small tremors beneath the earth's surface. We haven't detected the rising temperature and the increasing pressure. When the boiling, churning lava becomes too much to contain, it breaches the volcano and gushes forth, destroying everything in its path.

The youth are breaching the establishment. They are pushing against antiquated and nonsensical social norms and expectations. The internet acts as a powerful tool, providing a platform for youth to gather, share their values and gain accumulative force in their resistance. The push grows stronger and the lava is beginning to flow.

Many of the elders—fearful of change they do not understand—are pushing back, fighting to retain the establishment they have created. This may not be the best defensive tactic for, as blogger Alexander Beiner warns, "The more we repress ideas, the more they will breach."[3]

The greater the resistance, the stronger the buildup of pressure, and the more dramatic the explosion.

Beiner goes on to describe the concept of breaching as it relates specifically to social change.

"Breach is what happens when a collective intelligence birthed online bursts into the physical world and permanently changes its foundation… Breach is a sign that the barrier holding back our collective imagination is fracturing and will, at some point, dissolve."

> *One day our generation*
> *Is going to rule the population*

---

3   "The Age of Breach: Gamestop, Wokeism and The Capitol Riot," (Alexander Beiner, January 29, 2021), https://medium.com/rebel-wisdom/the-age-of-breach-gamestop-wokeism-and-the-capitol-8e3ac46efaf9.

Youth are organizing and demanding change—in their home lives, in their work lives and as global citizens of this world. They are done waiting on the world to change. They are gathering in like-minded tribes and going to war for what they believe in. They are ready to breach. It has already begun.

What if, instead of resisting what we may not understand, we open the door and usher in change? What if we use our roles as elders to empower the youth to make this world a better place?

Admittedly, writing it, and speaking it, is exponentially easier than *doing* it. That's why I chose not to alter the content of this book. From beginning to end, you may feel a shift in tone as I wrestle with my own identity as an elder and leader of our youth.

> What if we use our roles as elders to empower the youth to make this world a better place?

I want you to know that my journey in writing this book, reconceptualizing leadership and restructuring my company was incredibly uncomfortable. It forced me to take an honest look at myself and my values. Despite these growing pains, I came out the other side a better person. I want that for you, too, and so I encourage you to read this book with an open mind toward the possibilities and potential of youth's desire

not for a different type of leader, but for a leaderless society.

CHAPTER THREE
YOUTHFUL AMBITION

GROWING INTO MYSELF

I was born in a small mining town in South Africa in August 1975. In the seventies, Springs was a lovely suburban oasis, which is approximately fifty kilometers (a sixty minute drive) from Johannesburg. While our house didn't have a white picket fence, this visual is the perfect representation of the lifestyle my family lived. My parents, Mervyn and Molly, gave my siblings and I Hebrew names—my older sister Gila, younger sister Yael and myself, Ronen. In a town where Afrikaans was the predominant language, no one could pronounce our names properly, which made me bubble with both laughter and frustration. For the first twenty years of my life, I answered to two names—my proper name, which my family called me, RoNEN—and the public mispronunciation of my name, ROnen.

As a child, I could be described as easygoing, fun and caring—though I was a quirky child—an old soul perhaps, or just the product of being a middle child. For as long as I can remember, I felt different. It was as if I were an adult trapped in the body of a child, and I craved the freedom I thought my ancient wisdom deserved. I was often on my own, essentially raising myself, but was confident in who I was.

I was a popular child, well-liked by others, and was confident in some respects, but shy in others—especially with the girls. I think they could sniff out my insecurities. I attended a small school, which had one class per grade. As I reached sixth grade, the tides unexpectedly turned. Suddenly, and for reasons which I cannot discern, I was bullied and mocked by the girls in my class. Perhaps it was the result of my being different and the coming of age when differences matter. Assimilation is a survival skill in middle school and I did not dress the same, act the same or think the same as my classmates—perhaps a result of my small town upbringing. Not that I wanted to anyway. One day I was popular and the next I was seen as a social leper—ignored, teased and shunned. By seventh grade, I was back on top—I excelled in academics & athletics and became head boy. In retrospect, I wonder if I peaked too soon

While some level of bullying may seem like a common symptom of pre-adolescence for many—for me, it was a defining moment in my early development. This unfair mistreatment created a lifelong aversion to conflict. Or, perhaps I was born with this aversion. Regardless, because of this deep discomfort, my romantic relationships never lasted more than a month. I would turn and flee as soon as things became uncomfortable, scary or difficult. At the hint of a first fight with any girl I was dating, I would be gone. All because of something that happened when I was twelve years old.

Luckily, I was blessed with a fresh start in high school when I attended King David Linksfield, a Jewish boarding school in Johannesburg. This place seemed like heaven, a safe space where I could grow into my essence. I was liked by my teachers and I knew it—often using my charm to my advantage. I could be naughty and get away with it because everyone thought I was so sweet..

In tenth grade, I had the privilege of studying in Israel for three months. Seeing the world and travelling without my parents changed me indelibly. This trip became my social breach, the launching pad into a new version of myself. I was able to break free of my insecurities and finally begin feeling like the man I knew I was destined to become.

After high school I enrolled at University of the Witwatersrand in Johannesburg, studying economics, commerce and psychology. (I often joke that I studied psychology to understand why I was studying accounting.) The unusual combination of these subject areas was a result of my natural curiosity, but turned into a game-changing experience for me.

GROWING OUT OF THE FAMILY BUSINESS

Many years ago, my grandparents separately immigrated to South Africa from Lithuania, after escaping the Russians and

Nazis in WWII. Both having very limited English capabilities, a shared traumatic experience—and no sense of safety—their similar stories drew them together upon meeting in South Africa. Eventually, my grandfather learned to speak the local dialect and opened a small shop where he supplied bikes and spare parts to the miners in Springs. After some success, my grandfather branched out and began importing toys, a wise business decision at the time.

From the time I was ten years old, I spent my weekends working at the family business. It was, essentially, a lifelong internship. While I can look back with gratitude for the skills I developed during this time, as a child, I felt nothing but resentment for the responsibility and burden I carried at such a young age. I felt immense pressure to contribute and had notably less freedom than my friends. Even in retrospect, it feels as if I was robbed of a carefree childhood.

By the time I graduated from university, it was expected that I would be the third generation to run the family business. It was very clear that my future had been mapped out for me and that I was being groomed to take over once my grandfather and father reached retirement age. Unfortunately, I knew my destiny lay elsewhere. I knew that I was destined to do significant work in the world, that I couldn't spend my life in Springs—however, I couldn't put my finger on what that work would actually look like. I simply knew what it *wasn't*.

My father understood. While he certainly wanted me to join the family legacy, he would never force me. In his youth my father had different dreams. During the seventies when my father expressed concerns similar to my own—his longing to carve his own path—he considered moving to the United States, a dream that was put on hold by the Vietnam War. If he immigrated, he would most likely be drafted as a soldier. My grandfather seized this opportunity, delivering the ultimatum that, if my father stayed in South Africa, he would be expected to join the family business. Whether he knew it at the time or not, my father resigned himself to the fact that this would be his only career decision for the rest of his working life.

It was in a university course that I first began to question my family's way of doing business, realizing their processes and ideas were antiquated and even backward. My grandfather was old school and refused the possibility of change. He valued tradition and his comfort zone. Innovation was irritating and unnecessary. My father however, shared my interest in new ways of thinking and doing business. While his mind was open to possibility, his apprehension kept him static. He knew things needed to change, but felt he was not equipped to make it happen. He needed help and wanted me to do it. So, there we were, in a multi-generational battle—the old, the transition and the new.

As you will come to find out in this book, I am currently embroiled in a similar battle myself. Ironically, at this moment, I stand in my father's shoes—knowing changes must be made but feeling held back by fear. The beautiful blessing of the uncomfortable situation I find myself in is that I am full of empathy for my father as I see the parallels in our journeys. It's hard to let go of the way we are used to doing things.

With one foot in the family business and one foot out the door I knew I needed to buy myself some time. While I didn't quite know what my future held, I knew exactly what I *didn't* want. I was ready to walk away from the business, but couldn't quite see the vision of my future laid out before me. Everything was blurry. In an effort to gain some valuable work experience outside of what I already knew, I decided to interview with an investment banker. He asked, "Where do you see yourself in five years, Ronen?"

I almost laughed. Five years seemed like a lifetime! (I also didn't want to tell him that there was no way I'd still be at the bank in five years.)

"I don't know where I'll be in one year," I replied honestly. "But, I do know that I have a huge amount of potential. Just give me an opportunity and I'll show you."

When he informed me that I had neither the seniority nor experience to become an investment banker, I was not phased. "We only have menial administrative work for you," he explained.

What the banker didn't know was that my friend's father used to run the canteen in that very bank. When the workers would go on strike, my friend's father would call upon us to act as waiters and dishwashers. "I've done menial work before. This, in fact, would be a promotion!"

The job was mine and I spent the next three years working hard and learning as much as I could. I loved it, but there came a point when I realized that if I stayed, this job would give me no control over my future. When I looked left and right, I realized that bankers were not my tribe. I was beginning to realize that I was an entrepreneur, not an employee. As I grew to accept that I had an issue with authority, I wondered if I was actually employable at all!

I was twenty-five years old, outwardly achieving success, but inwardly miserable. It seemed my choices were either to remain at the bank or to take over the family business. My heart was in neither option and I knew the longer I stayed in this job, the more likely it was that I would abandon my dreams.

As young people do, I decided that the cure to my unhappiness was not deep introspection, but a vacation. So, I travelled to a famous location in South Africa, called Tsitsikamma for a five-day hike in the wilderness named the Otter Trail. On the second day, I found myself hanging out at the most gorgeous river crossing. I was relaxing, laughing and surrounded by friends when a lightning bolt of clarity hit me—when I returned from this trip, I needed to resign from the bank. This new knowledge was the beginning of a chain reaction where things started to fall into place.

Over the previous months, I had been meeting a friend of mine at the canteen. His name was Jason Glick, a college buddy who was consulting at the bank. We'd order toast with peanut butter, drink cappuccinos and swap stories of misery, of selling out to the corporate world. In his last year at university, Jason—who was studying to become an electrical engineer—had designed a website. On this particular day, as we sat reminiscing, the discussion of his website became a seed of inspiration for both of us. Suddenly, we could see the future.

That is the moment when I decided to take control of my life, to become the man I wanted to be. That is the moment when we started Student Village.

Suddenly, we could see the future.

CHAPTER FOUR
WHY YOUTH?

"This world demands the qualities of youth:
not a time of life but a state of mind, a temper
of the will, a quality of the imagination, a
predominance of courage over timidity, of the
appetite for adventure over the love of ease."
ROBERT F. KENNEDY

With change comes resistance. Each generation looks at the world their elders created, questioning the belief system they have inherited. Which parts are worth buying into? Which parts can they disregard? While each generation brings something new and innovative, the ones that came before them fight the change, resisting the destruction of what they know and value.

Tension is the only thing each generational shift has in common.

Youth is a necessary tool for evolution. They might come with a few bugs that need to be worked out, but they also come with an upgrade on previous factory settings. We need to constantly reinvent ourselves if we wish to stay relevant and to survive. As we age, this reinvention becomes more and more difficult as we get stuck in our ideas and our ways. Youth seem to adapt with greater ease and enthusiasm. They look at any given situation or expectation and do not feel the immediate need to conform. Instead, they question.

What doesn't make sense?
Why does it have to be done this way?
How do we do it better?

They ask without hesitation, reservation or judgment. It's inspiring. Sometimes as we get older, we hold hard and fast to our familiar ways of thinking and behaving. We cling to our values and ideologies as if there are no other options. When someone dares to suggest an alternative perspective, we become offended—as if our life's work was irrelevant. Youth don't mean to offend, they mean to explore, to improve and to expand.

Let's take a minute to explore this concept of change and resistance as it has played out through the last few decades.

YOUTH: AN AGENT OF CHANGE

Baby boomers (born between 1946-1964) grew up to shift traditional gender roles that had been around for centuries. They blew apart the time-honored tradition of men having the sole responsibility for the financial welfare of their family and women staying home to tend the house and kids. As baby boomer women enrolled in university and joined the workforce, marriages became equal partnerships. Men began doing chores, cooking and actively raising children.

Generation X (born between 1965-1980) is also known as the latch-key generation, and are the result of the new dual-income dynamic created by the baby boomers. With both parents at work, this generation of youth were often left to fend for themselves, either home alone or told to go out and play until the street lights came on. This freedom fostered an independent generation, youth who became creative problem solvers. Generation X became pioneers of technology, exploring the internet as the primary means of communication and exploring the world. They paved the way for society as we know it today.

Millennials (born between 1981-1996) are a generation with a reputation for being lazy and entitled. Raised by "helicopter parents" (moms and dads who hovered close and rushed in to protect their kids from failure, pain or adversity) this group of youth became infamous for an over-inflated sense of self-esteem. Millennials desired a work-life balance and refused to suffer the nine-to-five grind. They were the first generation to value their passions and hustled to turn them into careers.

Millennials are the transition generation between the status quo and disruptive change. Gen Xers and those who came before them measured their success in terms of productivity. *How busy are you? How stressed are you? How hard are you working? How much money are you making?* Millennials looked at this establishment and decided that they could not buy into such an exhausting, profit-chasing, and narrow-minded society. "Why must we work so hard?" they asked. "There is so much more to life than work," they said.

While this may sound like laziness, it's actually a cry for flexibility and freedom. The traditional nine-to-five work day, suit-and-tie lifestyle felt confining. Millennials craved a smarter, more efficient way of working. Their vision was to use technology to their advantage—allowing them to work from home and find freedom within their schedules, which meant time for other joys in life such as travel, friendship and fun. Millennials essentially looked at institutions that were broken, corrupt and inefficient and said, "No thank you. We see a better way of doing things." This attitude is bound to piss people off.

Millennials essentially arrived on the scene with a set of demands. I think those demands should be seen as suggestions for how we can reorganize the traditional workplace. I believe their message was right, but perhaps their delivery was abrupt and their timing was off. They were just too early.

The irony of the situation is, with Covid-19, when many of us have been forced to work from home, we have become exposed to the millennial way of life. We have come to appreciate the comfort and flexibility of working from our couches and have developed new routines that allow time for family and hobbies. After reluctantly being exposed to a new way of working and using technology to our advantage, many in the older generations have seen the value in the way of life the millennials have been pursuing. We now understand the benefits of balance between work and play, business and family, money and relaxation.

I had this realization as I sat on the couch dressed in my new "office attire"—an old t-shirt and a comfortable pair of shorts. I had my laptop balanced on my knees and Netflix humming in the background. I was running my business and attending a virtual conference at the same time, when I had a groundbreaking notion—we really could run the world from the couch! It turns out, the millennials were right.

Millennials, in their inherent acceptance of technology, are the first generation to form a larger tribe. They saw the internet as a gateway to the world and used it to create communities of like-minded people. They saw the possibilities presented when one is able to reach out on a worldwide scale. Employers were no longer drawing from the local talent pool, but could truly find the best and the brightest—regardless of location. Young adults who struggled to find others to understand their identity and their passions were able to connect with people who shared similar interests and stories. Businesses could learn from the successes and failures of their colleagues and competitors on a global scale. The definition of one's community no longer meant the boundaries of your town or neighborhood. Community was now a worldwide concept.

Thank you, millennials.

Eric Yuan, CEO of Zoom, echoed similar sentiments in terms of flexibility, adaptation and the necessity of passing the torch to the up-and-comers. He said, "Millennials grew up realizing they could get the job done without having to go to the office—sooner or later this is going to be the new normal because the world doesn't belong to us anymore."

Generation Z (born between 1996-2010) has inherited a messed up world. They have been handed a reality which is laden with political corruption and scandal, with racial resentment, with privileged mentality, with environmental crisis and with economic uncertainty. They are not blind to it. They see the injustice and are fighting to make change. Their natural ability to connect, to collaborate and to use technology to their advantage will serve them well in forming a large and powerful tribe on a global scale.

The millennials, full of ideals and values that we all eventually subscribed to, was a generation that was all about *me*. With their new software upgrades, Gen Z upholds those values, but with a wider scope. They are the *We* generation. Being the first generation to be born into a world immersed in technology (they don't know a time without a smartphone), these tech natives operate seamlessly in both the virtual and real world. They have learned that technology can be used to support meaningful causes, to gather a tribe of like-minded people, and to create disruptive change.

Generation Z will be the ones to truly change our world for the better. Mark my words. As a collective whole, this group of young people are becoming social justice warriors who are not only idealistic, but are organized and have a call to action. These are the people who will lead us to higher ground and they believe that the higher ground is meant for all of us. Not just the whites, not just the men, not just the Christians, not just the wealthy. Gen Z doesn't believe in salvation for a lucky few, but for every single one of us.

YOUTH AS FORTUNE TELLERS

If you want to know what's coming in the future, look toward the youth. Pay attention to teenagers because what's important to them will inevitably become what's important to the world—social justice, gender equality, capitalism—they are crystal balls for what is to come.

Young people shake up our traditional thinking and routine procedures. Though uncomfortable, this evolution is a necessary part of life. Think about it—traditional thinking is what allowed enslavement, apartheid and hate crimes based on sexual orientation. Someone had to stand up and lead society toward different values.

The world, as we know it, is chaotic— in a state of constant change, upheaval and surprise. We may try to predict the future but we certainly cannot control it. If we want to thrive in the midst of this chaos, we need to adhere to some guiding principles of evolution:

1. The ability to adapt
2. The ability to pivot with a moment's notice

3. The ability to find a sense of calm within the storm

4. The ability to connect

I hate to break it to you but the more we resist the necessity of change, the more chaos we will create. The more resistance, the greater the breach. Pushing back against change will not only exhaust you, but will render you irrelevant and stressed out. Yes, change is uncomfortable. It requires effort and an open mind, but change could very well lead to a better version of you and your business.

> If you want to know what's coming in the
> future, look toward the youth.

One of the most fascinating things about youth, in my opinion, is that they seem to come with these evolutionary principles pre-programmed in their settings. They didn't have to learn these principles through difficult life lessons. These characteristics are embedded in their programming. They didn't have to learn these things—adaptation, pivoting, balance and connection. These characteristics are innate to our youth.

As elders, it is our job to push aside not the suggestion of change, but to push aside our own egos. We need to admit that though the message of the youth may not always be delivered with wisdom, grace or tact, it is a message worth considering. Change is good. Change is necessary. Change equals evolution.

Every generation has a purpose. Every generation brings change in their wake.

Exponential change is the result of generational disruption of strongly-held ideas and norms. If the elders were left to their own devices, they would rely solely on the knowledge and beliefs they have collected over the years. This would result in slow, steady incremental change in their society. Would they create growth? Yes, most likely. Would it be effective? Probably not. With the disruptive energy of the youth—who question, challenge, and call for re-imagining—come prime opportunities for exponential change and powerful, uncomfortable (but necessary) growth. This is the primary role of each new generation, to create inevitable disruption and usher in a new way of thinking and living.

Even if it's not convenient.
Even if it's not what you wanted.
Even if it's not what the elders ordered.
Because it's what the world needs in order to grow.

CHAPTER FIVE
GENERATION Z

Before we dive into the crux of the book, it's important to take a moment and clarify who exactly we are discussing. When you read or hear the term "youth", you may assume it refers to anyone younger than yourself. If you are in your sixties, youth may be those "kids" in their forties. If you are in your forties, you may conjure up images of fresh-faced, wrinkle-free twenty year olds. It's all relative, really.

In recent years, the most infamous youth generation were the millennials (those kids raised by late boomers and early Generation Xers) who gained a reputation for being unmotivated, whiny and entitled. They perfected the hipster image—an intentionally haphazard look—women who squeezed themselves into yoga pants were not the only ones balancing messy buns atop their heads. Men, too, fashioned "man buns," which were accentuated by ironic lumberjack beards.

This book will certainly reference the millennials, for this group of young people paved the way for Generation Z, just as those who came before paved the way for us. We will unpack possible truths and stereotypes about them, just as we will for those in Generation Z. For the purpose of this book, however, our passing references to the millennials will simply be to set the stage for our present youth. At the time I write this book, the millennial generation have become young adults—ranging from twenty-three to thirty-nine years old. They are stepping into leadership roles, raising children and beginning to mentor those who follow in their footsteps. Soon, they will accept the torch passed to them by baby boomers and Gen Xers to fulfill the role of village elders. I hate to say their time to make an impact as young and impressionable youth has come and gone, but—I fear their time has come and gone. The millennials had lofty aspirations but none of the gumption necessary to follow through and make those ideas a reality. It may or may not be their fault (which we can discuss in later pages).

My fascination with Generation Z stems from my excitement over their tendency to take action at a very young age. While millennials talked the talk, in terms of global change, Gen Z are already walking the walk. This seems like an opportune time for those of us who are young elders to be mindful about how we are coaching, shaping and supporting our youth so that they may go forth with wisdom—as well as enthusiasm—to make great change.

GEN Z: A GLOBAL TRIBE

Gen Z is not only the first generation to be born within technology (they do not know life without a smartphone or the internet), but they are also the most ethnically diverse group of youth we have seen. Almost half of this generation is made up of minorities.[4] These two mitigating factors matter, for it is what has allowed Gen Z to adopt a global consciousness based upon acceptance. Not tolerance, but true acceptance.

Generation Z sees the whole world as its tribe, and this mentality has affected the way they think, congregate and work. They have adopted a collaborative approach to accomplishing their goals—seeking connection based on shared purpose and passion. They do not feel the need for a hierarchy, as they value the contribution of individual knowledge and skill sets to get the job done. Their foundation is built upon trust and mutual respect, and a high level of buy-in churns out effective results.

This collaborative mentality is significant in that there has been a fundamental change, not only in corporate structuring, but in the approaches taken toward problem solving and innovation. In a future chapter, I will introduce the concept of Design Thinking, a profound and effective mindset that will inevitably revolutionize the way this world functions and

---

4   "Generation Z News Latest Characteristics, Research, And Facts," (Business Insider, 2021), https://www.businessinsider.com/generation-z?r=AU&IR=T.

governs. For now, I would simply like to provide a sneak peek and hint at Gen Z's enormous potential for global change.

Exposure to other's perspectives, ideals and ways of living, coupled with large-scale ethnic diversification is what has created a generational culture of love for one another and hatred for intolerance. Generation Z is the first group of youth to openly celebrate individuality. Are you bi-racial? No problem! Gay? You love who you love! Transgender? Let your light shine! Unwed parent? How can we support you? Not only do they accept and celebrate, but they are willing to break down barriers previously indoctrinated by generations that came before them.

This generation is able to hold radical ideas and facilitate change because they are too young to fully understand the realm of politics. And, they don't let that stop them. In fact, their naivety can be seen as a strength, for they are not drawn into political games, lobbyist corruption or the need for power. They are simply chasing what is right and just.

Whereas the millennials held many of these same idealistic values (but were unmotivated to take action), Gen Z is willing to mobilize.

They use the internet as a tool to gather and make change by organizing rallies, marches and petitions. They engage in meaningful discussions online and are not afraid to call people out for antiquated, privileged or bigoted opinions. This group of youth is putting their money where their mouth is, taking action and forcing society to evolve.

SHINING EXAMPLES OF THE GEN Z SPIRIT

Greta Thunberg

Born in 2003, this Swedish environmental activist is far from your average young person. At the ripe old age of fifteen, Greta Thunberg chose to spend her days standing outside of the Swedish parliament building, criticizing world leaders for their failure to address climate change. While it was certainly a topic of global conversation, Thunberg felt not enough action was being taken and she was unafraid to take on world powers to fight for what she felt was right and just.

Following her 2018 address at the United Nations Climate Change Conference, large scale student-led protests were held around the world. Millions of youth were standing up for their beliefs and gaining international attention for it.

In her 2019 speech at the United Nations Climate Action Summit, Thunberg was unafraid to call out the establishment for their lack of action on the environmental crisis, scolding, "How dare you!", a comment that made policy makers uncomfortable enough to attack with condescension—typical of those whose authority is threatened. US president Donald Trump felt compelled to address Greta on Twitter, writing, "So ridiculous. Greta must work on her Anger Management problem, then go to a good old fashioned movie with a friend! Chill Greta, Chill!"

This response elicited a viral conversation and endless content for comical memes portraying Greta as a heroine who was willing to stick it to "The Man" and used Trump as a villainous symbol of the establishment. Ironically, Trump's reaction only fueled support for Greta's environmental causes.

To date, Greta has been nominated for two Nobel Peace Prizes (2019, 2020) for her leadership efforts. She continues to act with courage and determination, inspiring others to rise up against government indifference.

Ben Pasternak

At age twenty-one, this Australian-born entrepreneur has combined his love of chicken nuggets with his passion for environmental sustainability, resulting in the creation of a vegan version of his favorite snack, Nuggs. Selling his product online, Ben has managed to create a business that is on track to earn $8 million in 2021.

Mohamad Al Jounde

At a very young age, Mohamad Al Jounde (born in 2001) fled his home country of Syria and became a refugee in Lebanon. For the first two years of his new life living in a refugee camp, Mohamad could not attend school. Instead of letting this struggle deter his enthusiasm for learning, he decided to enlist his mother's help and they began to build a school with their own hands.

By the age of twelve, Mohamad was teaching math and photography to other refugee children, reminding them of the importance of pursuing an education. When the government decided to dismantle the camp—subsequently destroying Mohamad's school—he simply chose to build another one. Today, Mohamad's school has a professional teaching staff and educates approximately 200 students.

Awarded the International Children's Peace Prize in 2017 at the age of 16, Mohamad chose to use this platform as an effective way to raise awareness about the lives of refugee children.

Xiaoyin Qu

Listed in the "Forbes 30 Under 30" list for 2021, Xiaoyin Qu founded her online professional events company, Run the World, one month before Covid-19 forced cancellations all around the globe. A worldwide shift toward online conferences and events, coupled with Xiaoyin's foresight and tenacity, has grown her company from five to forty-five employees in its first year. Run the World has hosted over 10,000 events to date.

Emma Gonzalez

This brave young woman, born in 1999, was a senior at Marjory Stoneman Douglas High School in Fort Lauderdale, Florida, on the day a gunman burst into her school and killed seventeen people.

After witnessing the cold-blooded murder of her classmates, friends and teachers, Emma Gonzalez decided to stand up and call out a government that seemed to place value on the right to carry arms over the safety and security of innocent children.

Mere days after the shooting, Gonzalez spoke publicly, sharing her concerns, saying, "We are standing together because if all our government and president can do is send thoughts and prayers, then it's time for victims to be the change we need to see."[5]

This public shaming of the government was received by youth, who joined Gonzalez in expressing rage and disappointment toward their elders. On February 20, 2018, several students who survived the Florida shooting addressed the Florida State Legislature, advocating for stronger gun control laws. The next day, they rallied and spoke at an internationally televised town hall meeting. Shortly thereafter, Emma Gonzalez aired her concerns on Twitter and gained more than one million followers in less than ten days. Youth all over the country were standing behind her, in support of her message.

Since 2018, Emma Gonzalez has co-founded a gun control advocacy group called Never Again MSD.

Miranda Wang and Jeanny Yao

These twenty-six year old friends used their shared environmental interests as inspiration to found their company BioCellection. Miranda and Jeanny invented a chemical

---

5   "Florida student Emma Gonzalez to lawmakers and gun advocates: 'We call BS'," (CNN Staff, February 18, 2018), https://edition.cnn.com/2018/02/17/us/florida-student-emma-gonzalez-speech/index.html.

technology that breaks down unrecyclable plastic into valuable base chemicals. For every ton of plastic trash, more than $2,500 worth of chemicals can be created, saving our planet twenty tons of emitted carbon dioxide.

Malala Yousafzai

Born in Pakistan in 1997, Malala Yousafzai found herself in a world ruled by the Taliban and was forced to follow their strict code of conduct. Being raised by parents who valued education immensely, Malala rebelled when it was announced that girls could no longer attend school. At the age of eleven, Malala began to write a blog (using a pseudonym) that chronicled daily life under Taliban control.

Within a year, the blog began to gain attention and the young activist was asked to provide interviews in print and on television. She quickly became the face of disruption and was noticed by the Taliban.

In 2012, Malala was shot in the face by the Taliban, while on a bus with her friends. This aggressive action toward a child brought international condemnation upon this rebel group and was the beginning of the end for the Taliban regime.

Instead of being scared into silence, Malala continued to rise up against those who controlled her country. She wrote a bestselling autobiography, entitled *I am Malala* and created the Malala Fund, which advocates for female education around the world.

At the age of seventeen, Malala Yousafzai became the youngest Nobel Prize laureate for her efforts.

Ayakha Melithafa

Born in Cape Town, South Africa in 2002, Ayakha was one of sixteen teenage activists to file a complaint to the United Nations Committee on the Rights of the Child, addressing the climate crisis her generation has inherited.

Her passion for climate change has led her to become a recruitment official for the African Climate Alliance, as well as contributor to "Project 90 by 2030"—a South African organization committed to reducing carbon by 90%. She is a sought-after speaker and was invited to represent her country at the World Economic Forum in 2020.

Abraham M. Keita

Born in 1998—in the midst of Liberia's civil war—Abraham (also known as Keita) lost his father after he was shot in an ambush when Keita was five years old. As a result, his family grew up in extreme poverty, surrounded by death, disease and violence.

When he was nine years old, a thirteen year old girl from Keita's community was raped and murdered. Appalled by the news, he decided to attend a peaceful protest in hopes of bringing his neighbor's murderer to justice. Fellow protesters, who were impressed by the young boy's passion, invited him to join the Liberian Children's Parliament, where Keita went on to organize marches encouraging the government to respect children's rights.

In 2012, Keita and his fellow advocates celebrated the signing of the Children's Act and successfully lobbied for national funding for free schooling for all children.

Keita was awarded the International Children's Peace Prize in 2017, at seventeen years old.

In recent years, he has become a member of The Kids Rights Youngsters, a youth-led advocacy group who engage local children to act locally, influence policy, and speak out to world leaders. He also has a popular weekly radio program (#OurFuture)—a platform he uses to discuss issues affecting children in Liberia and all over the world.

Amanda Gorman

This young American poet (born in 1998) walked into the international spotlight when she shared a poem that stunned her audience into emotional silence at President Joe Biden's inauguration ceremony in January of 2021. While many of us had not heard her name before that moment, she had already been writing for years—publishing a collection of poems as early as 2015. Through written and spoken word, Amanda Gorman is using her platform to raise awareness on topics such as oppression, feminism, race, and marginalization and is engaging audiences of all ages in meaningful conversation.

Caleb Annobil

Caleb Annobil became passionate about clean water after watching his friend die of cholera. While still in high school, Caleb partnered with a friend and the two of them began thinking about solutions to a worldwide problem. As a result, they created High School Water, an enterprise which customises sachets of water to be sold at affordable prices.

As acting CEO, Caleb has the goal of propelling his team toward becoming the main water dealer in Ghana. To date, he has a consumer base of over 1.5 million students and employs over 250 African youth.

WHAT DOES THIS MEAN?

All of the social justice warriors listed above have many attributes in common.

1. They see injustice and choose to take action
2. They believe in the power one person has to make a difference
3. They are not limited by their age or lack of experience
4. They have supportive adults in their lives

Youth often have grandiose ideas, for they are unencumbered by negative life experience, political constraints or societal expectation. They believe in their own power and are not hindered by their lack of knowledge. These lofty plans often begin in early childhood. Ask any young child what they want to be when they grow up and they will most likely list more than one occupation. They want to be a doctor, a fashion designer *and* an astronaut. They simply don't know yet that it can't be done. We let them dream because we don't want to be the one who places a ceiling on their aspirations and we have faith that life will sort it out, sooner or later.

Yet, at a certain age, we start to do just that—we place a ceiling on their goals and scoff at their passions. *You can't challenge the system. It's like David versus Goliath! You can't eradicate racism. It's too deeply ingrained.* At what age do we begin to burst their ambitious bubbles? At what age do we begin telling our youth that their ambitions are unattainable, unreasonable and unrealistic? Often youth are standing up against what we all know is wrong—their enthusiastic innocence makes them brave enough to speak out while we seethe in silence. Which is worse?

So often, we shake our heads at their lack of experience. *They just don't understand. Wait until they're older and they'll get it. They'll be eaten alive.* Maybe this lack of experience is not necessarily a detriment, but a positive attribute. Maybe this youthful lack of understanding is what allows them to be courageous, to attempt the unthinkable. As young elders, we should be encouraging their passions and cheering them on as they stand up against the establishment, break down barriers and cry out for what we all know is right and just. We can advise them, provide some wisdom, pick them up when they fall, dust them off and tell them to keep going.

Innocent, passionate hearts coupled with patient wisdom is a recipe for success.

A supportive adult seems to be a key element. Malala Yousafzai had a father who encouraged her to pursue an education despite the Taliban's rules and who stood beside her at every interview, every speech. Mohamad Al Jounde's mother helped him build schools brick by brick. These young people are proving that one person who takes action can affect millions—yet that one person also needs someone. That's the beauty of it. As an elder, you can affect change by acting as a motivator, by acknowledging youth and youthful ambition. The one person who creates change needs one person to believe in them.

Whether the adult is a parent, a teacher, an employer or a mentor, youth often require someone who can guide them, focus their energy and provide the benefit of experience. As the powerfully passionate educator Rita Pierson declares in her motivational TED Talk—"every kid needs a champion"[6]—someone who believes in their potential and stands beside them in challenging situations.

I hope, in reading this book, you will begin to discover the inherent value of grandiose dreams, naivety and innocence. I hope you will consider youth in your life, your family

---

6   "Every Kid Needs a Champion," (Rita Pierson, May 2013), https://www.ted.com/talks/rita_pierson_every_kid_needs_a_champion?language=en.

and your work and begin to think about how you can be a champion for them.

However, being able to effectively champion youth—to lead, support and guide them—requires us to set aside our egos. We need to look inward and admit that perhaps we have misunderstood youth and mislabeled their differences as negativities. Perhaps youthful traits that make us uncomfortable are evolutionary adaptations necessary to survive a rapidly changing world. Perhaps if the older generations fail to embrace what we don't yet understand, this will be our death sentence. *We'll* be eaten alive.

We often find ourselves pointing fingers and lecturing youth. However, our knowledge and experience—while potentially helpful—does not exempt us from doing our own work. The finger pointing goes both ways. We discredit younger generations and they discredit us. We are all required to grow. I might even go as far as to suggest that elders need to practice resurrection—a constant cycle of dying and being reborn in our expectations, our reality and our hopes for the future.

> Perhaps youthful traits that make us uncomfortable are evolutionary adaptations necessary to survive a rapidly changing world.

As we dive into the next **section** of the book, I encourage you to read with an open and honest heart, and ask yourself which of these stereotypes you subscribe to. We all subscribe to one stereotype or another. It's a natural response to actions and beliefs that are different from our own and that we may not fully comprehend. Once a stereotype is uncovered, letting go of our preconceptions is the only way to pave the path for growth.

You may begin by remembering stereotypes that held you back in your own youth—those that kept you from feeling heard, acknowledged and validated. How many of those notions were true? How many were simply the result of misunderstood intentions? How many of those myths resulted in you feeling judged and led to a resentment that blocked your desire for connection? Maybe remembering your own youthful experiences will allow you to feel the gravity of the beliefs you hold.

People easily get stuck in the misconception that their truth is *the* truth. Our experiences shape our reality and we forget the subjectivity of it. Our experiences are often colored by emotional nostalgia—which may taint the accuracy of our memories. We might say, "When I was a student, I was wiser, more responsible. The world was a better place." In reality, we were drinking beer in our dorm rooms and eating discount noodles because we were broke.

As elders, we need to review our own stigmas and break through the limits our own experiences have placed upon us. We need to open ourselves to the possibility of a different truth, to allow space for different opinions and perspectives. We need to recognize that our own experience does not represent the collective whole and we need to let curiosity broaden our understanding.

With curiosity, we experience a richer, deeper version of life and we open up the spectrum of possibility. This is the lens through which we should look at youth.

SECTION 2:

DISPELLING THE MYTHS

CHAPTER SIX
DISPELLING THE MYTHS

Have you ever had a moment when the words that come out of your mouth surprise you—for they sound exactly like something your mother or father would have said?

"When I was your age..."
"You youngsters have it so easy..."
"Your priorities are all wrong..."
"Those entitled, lazy..."

We cringe when those judgmental words of misunderstanding and frustration escape our lips because they instantly age us in a way we weren't ready for. Those words and the misunderstanding are symbolic of the fact that we are no longer youthful. As discussed in the introduction of this book, a certain level of finger-wagging and hair-pulling seems to be a rite of passage. Generational gaps are natural, for change can often be misinterpreted as disrespect for those who fought hard to earn advances, imagine technology and create the current luxuries we all enjoy.

As we fight our knee-jerk reaction to respond with condescension, it's helpful to recognize that our relationship with youth is reciprocal. It's an equal exchange. For the gift of our wisdom, we receive a dose of fresh thinking, an invigorating energy and some enthusiasm. When we acknowledge the value each party has to offer, it becomes easier to learn from one another and to move forth with collaborative spirit.

In order for this symbiotic relationship to be successful, there needs to be open communication. It's up to the elders to create a safe space for this. If we want young people to communicate and be willing to listen—as well as share— they need to feel they are not being judged or misunderstood. For the elders to release judgement, we need to let go of (or try to reframe) our thinking in terms of the stereotypes we hold.

In this chapter, we will take a closer look at some of the myths surrounding youth. We will investigate the root cause of those misconceptions and I will try to provide new perspectives, which may help you consider the youth in a new way.

Stereotypes. Myths. We've all heard them. We've probably said them. Now let's dive right in and deconstruct them.

As we move into the next few chapters, you will notice I have written them in two opposing voices. The first, a voice of condescension, misunderstanding and judgment—fleeting thoughts or deep remnants that many elders have held at one point or another. The second, an attempt to share an alternate perspective, a plea for understanding and acceptance.

MYTH 1:

Youth Lack Patience and Loyalty

When you get a new piece of technology, sometimes the most frustrating thing is trying to figure out the software upgrades. While we are excited to have a new gadget and logically understand that the upgrades will serve us, we are used to doing things a certain way. Upgrades take time to understand and most of us dislike change. We need to battle our emotions in order to make progress.

In this chapter, we will investigate the myth that youth lack patience and loyalty. It certainly appears this way on the surface but what if, what looks like a lack of values may actually be a software upgrade?

MYTH: YOUTH LACK PATIENCE AND LOYALTY

It seems as if we are raising entire generations of young people who suffer from Attention Deficit Hyperactive Disorder

(ADHD)! The best you will ever get from them is their continual partial attention. Kids these days bounce around from activity to activity, job to job, girlfriend to girlfriend, boyfriend to boyfriend, and friend group to friend group. They can't even decide on a sports team to follow, jumping on the bandwagon only when things get exciting. Why can't they make a commitment and stick to it, like so many die-hard soccer fans and their teams?

Older generations value loyalty and commitment as if they were one of the Ten Commandments. Many baby boomers dedicated their entire careers to working for one company and were dismissed upon retirement—with a cake, a gold watch and a hearty thank you for their loyalty. It was not uncommon to hear of someone who worked thirty or forty years in one place. Happiness and fulfillment were not as important as earning a reliable income in order to support your family. People were simply grateful to have a steady job. If you were able to climb the corporate ladder and gain a little prestige, that was the cherry on top of the ice cream sundae.

Beginning with Generation X, and becoming progressively more fluid with each generation, switching jobs and careers became common practice. Kids quit subjects at school and leave jobs because they are boring, because it interferes with their extracurricular activities, because they want to try something new, or because they aren't advancing quickly enough. Young people don't work toward mastery. They are seeking novelty—ticking boxes on life's to-do list. It seems that millennials, especially, expected to walk straight out of college into a six-figure management position—CEO from day one. They were not willing to put in the necessary time to earn a respectful reputation and gather precious knowledge, experience and skills.

Youth are not only quitting their jobs, but they are also quitting their marriages. Globally, the divorce rate more than doubled between the years 1970 to 2008, from 2.6 divorces for every 1,000 married people to 5.5.[7]

Statistics specific to the United States show that 50% of marriages ended in divorce or separation in the year 2019.[8] Why is this happening? Does no one take their marriage vows seriously anymore?

It seems the younger generations view marriage as something that ebbs and flows, comes and goes, not as a commitment that should last a lifetime. Perhaps it is because they want to live the romantic wedding fantasy but are unprepared for the work that follows. As soon as life gets difficult or unpredictable, couples decide to break up and move on. In fact, it's very rare nowadays, to come across a younger couple who has been married for more than ten years. The result of this lack

---

7   "Divorce Rates Around the World: A Love Story" (Bella DePaulo, February 3, 2019), https://www.psychologytoday.com/ca/blog/living-single/201902/divorce-rates-around-the-world-love-story.

8   "Divorce Statistics: Over 115 Studies, Facts And Rates For 2020" (Wilkinson & Finkbeiner), https://www.wf-lawyers.com/divorce-statistics-and-facts/.

of matrimonial loyalty is that, within the last decade, the traditional makeup of a nuclear family (mom, dad, biological children), has been decimated, replaced by a society which no longer has rules or expectations when it comes to family structure.

Youth's tendency for instant gratification in terms of work and love has led to a chronic lack of patience. Everything has become so easy, so tangible and at-your-fingertips that people rarely need to leave the house anymore. Effort seems like a skill of the past. Generation Z, especially, are children of convenience. Want something to eat? You don't even need to place a phone call to have your pizza delivered! Click the app on your phone and Uber Eats will deliver it to your door in thirty minutes or less. No groceries? Ordering them online will save you from the tedious jobs of standing in line and bagging your produce. Again, they will be delivered right to your doorstep. Need something else? Toothbrush? New socks? A power drill? Amazon Prime will bring it to you in less than twenty-four hours.

And then, there's Siri and Alexa. You don't even need to Google anything.

You can simply ask the mystical, all-knowing artificial intelligence robot living in your house or on your phone.

It will even turn off the lights, turn up the heat, turn down the music or turn on the television. And, television! Kids don't even know what a commercial is anymore. They don't even know what television is. They watch whatever is on their device. We used to fight over the remote control. Now the fight is over the number of household users attempting to access Netflix simultaneously.

Perish the thought of something malfunctioning and youth must either a) learn to fix it b) wait for an appointment to have it fixed or c) do it themselves. They simply do not possess the patience required for basic problem solving. Disaster strikes when the Wifi goes down and they are unable to YouTube a fix! Does any of this sound familiar?

WHAT LIES BENEATH THE SURFACE

At first glance, it can be said that the younger generations lack both loyalty and patience. I agree with you, but what if we were to remove any negative language and investigate how these habits are *serving* youth?

The younger generations seem to place a profound emphasis on their own happiness. Staying in a job or a marriage that makes them unhappy is an antiquated way of thinking. All aspects of life have become more fluid and nothing is considered permanent. This may stem from the fact that they have been raised in a world where things change at a breakneck speed— technology, career options, political climate, economic booms and busts, and family structure. Above all else, these kids have had to learn to adapt and become resilient. Perhaps the ADHD mindset we previously referred to is actually built specifically for this—the ability to analyze, to consider multiple perspectives and to make quick decisions.

This skill—decisive and courageous decision-making—can be seen in the transactional way in which youth move from job to job. We may mistake this constant motion as disloyalty, when in fact it is a desire not only for challenge, but for an alignment of values. This generation has a mindset of constantly evaluating and adjusting. If something isn't working, they fix it, they try something new. Why stay in a job that is going nowhere, that isn't fulfilling, that doesn't meet your lifestyle needs, that doesn't allow for societal contribution when there are so many other options out there?

> What if we were to remove any negative language and investigate how these habits are serving youth?

As we saw during Covid-19, the ability to pivot on a moment's notice was invaluable. It made the difference between the companies who were able to survive (and perhaps thrive), and those who went bankrupt. Life and work can be unpredictable. When we are not tied down to an idea—or by loyalty, tradition or belief—it makes room for open-mindedness and innovative thinking. Things are constantly changing and Generation Z seems to have an innate preparedness for this reality. Sometimes, elders may be too stuck in our ways to see other possibilities.

In fact, in a recent South African report, youth were given the credit they were due, with the report stating, "The post-pandemic, new world order, which the world will struggle to adapt to, is what Gen Zs have been waiting for. As the first generation of true digital natives, the courage of their convictions will converge into a potent force that will reengineer the old world order in the next decade."[9]

This generation of self-directed, motivated, inspired young adults is poised to make change in a time when the world desperately needs it. What if their ADHD tendencies are not a deficit, but are in fact, their superpower—the quality that enables them to thrive in such a fast-paced world? While there have been many advances in ADHD research and treatment—the FDA has just approved a video game to help harness focusing abilities in youth—could it be that most of us are missing the point? We are trying to parent the ADHD out of young people, when perhaps, we should be asking what we can learn from their unique abilities.

On a final note, the lack of patience and the need for instant gratification displayed by our youth may actually not be entirely their fault. I ask you to consider how these children were raised. (We will discuss helicopter parenting in a future chapter.) Very few of them were allowed autonomy or control over their choices. These kids have spent their whole lives being served—their shoelaces tied, zippers zipped, backpacks carried and butts wiped. They have had their clothes, courses and activities chosen for them. They were given the best

---

9   "Generation Z – A Flux Trends Report," (Flux Trends, June 2020), https://www.fluxtrends.com/downloads/generation-z-flux-trends-report/.

toys, the coolest vacations and the shiniest cars. Many youth want for nothing. Couple this upbringing with the advent of technology and it's no wonder they expect things to come easily to them.

WHAT DOES THIS MEAN?

The first thing we need to ask ourselves is, could it be that patience and loyalty are *our* values and not theirs?

Young people are much more transactional than we were raised to be. They are searching for careers and relationships that align with their core beliefs and values.

They are constantly assessing and asking, *"Does this suit me?"* and if not, they are quick to move on. This is not to say that we can grant them the benefits of patience and loyalty, but we cannot expect youth to embody those qualities in the same way we would. The most effective way to teach the qualities we value is to embrace them ourselves.

If we wish for youth to be more patient, tolerant, loyal or understanding, then this is the lens through which we must interact with them. We must lead with empathy. Consider the rapid pace of life that young people are expected to navigate. Is it possible that disloyalty and impatience could actually be youth's ability to keep up with a world that moves and changes quickly? Does loyalty get in the way of making decisions or seeing situations with clarity?

While validating and acknowledging this mentality, we can simultaneously remind young people that they can't move faster than nature. In other words, some things are meant to take time. We often think, *"I should be more established, further along, richer by now."* If the pace of reality doesn't move as quickly as their dreams, many young people are destined to live in disappointment. This is the moment to teach patience.

Before bestowing life lessons on youth, we must be mindful to pick our battles. Does it matter that your child cheers for a different football team every season? Probably not. Should we encourage them to try, fail and keep trying before they find something worth nurturing? Yes.

Loyalty to those who have been good to us, have supported and encouraged us is, indeed, a lesson we can share. This holds true in both personal and professional relationships. There is something to be said for trust and the ability to weather a storm together. Being true to your word and honoring a gentleman's handshake seem to be lost skills—ones that could use some resurrection. Alternatively though, young people seem to be much braver than we were when it comes to terminating a toxic relationship. They hold no qualms about walking away from something that doesn't serve them and stepping into the unknown with naive faith that better things will come along. This isn't, necessarily, a bad trait. Youth have more options—professionally, financially and personally—than many of the generations who preceded them. They have the luxury of choice and the right to exercise it. So, what appears to be disloyalty may actually be a desire for options.

Some may argue that youth overuse and abuse this luxury, jumping ship the moment a task or a relationship becomes difficult. This may be true. Maybe we can reframe this "deficiency" by asking ourselves if the decision to quit prematurely is fear-based. Do youth leave or abandon things because they feel inadequate in coping with the challenge that lays ahead? This could hold true for issues ranging from household tasks that require a certain skill, to jobs that require effort and risk-taking, to relationships that call for empathy and compromise. If these decisions are based in fear and are an avoidance tactic, our role (as elders), is to teach youth problem-solving skills and emotional regulation.

How do *we* handle ourselves when things get tough? What is our self-talk? Who is our support system? What resources are available to us? So often, youth are privy to the stress and adversity of those around them, but not to the coping strategies we use.[10] Imagine how helpful it would be if the elders became more transparent in how they solve problems that arise. If we modelled how we move through fear, frustration and impatience and youth were able to witness our eventual successes—perhaps this patience and persistence may inspire them to try something new, attempt something again, or hold on for just a little while longer.

---

10   "Raising Resilient Children: Parents and teachers working in partnership to empower the children in our lives," (Cleeve, Kelly, 2020.) Peter Lang Publishing. New York, NY.

Youth need to know that they have space to make mistakes and need to learn from them. The pressure to achieve perfection is not only exhausting, but crippling. If the elders demonstrated empathy and patience toward those in their tribe, perhaps youth would not only be willing to push through challenges, but would extend that same empathy and patience to others around them. No one is perfect—not your spouse, not your boss, and definitely not your sports team. Vulnerability leads to empathy, to the ability to see each other as authentic human beings. When elders and youth learn to see each other holistically, we remove expectation and begin to meet the other where they are at.

The second aspect we must consider is our judgment of the youthful desire for happiness.

Wouldn't we all like to be happier? Maybe we could take a cue from youth when it comes to personal fulfillment and balance. Why relegate ourselves to jobs that make us miserable when there could be different options?

Most of us were raised to grow up and find a job. We would hustle from nine to five, then explore our hobbies on weekends and vacations. Youth simply don't subscribe to this mentality. They don't aim to balance, but to integrate. They follow their passions and strive to make a living while fulfilling their purpose.

Perhaps youth's desire for happiness is not a selfish and self-centered behavior, but is common sense and a method for sustainable productivity and inspiration? No one can be the best version of themselves when they are resentful or burnt out. Just because the elders of the past used loyalty and obligation as a measuring stick of self-worth (staying in boring jobs and bad marriages) doesn't mean it was the right thing to do. Instead of judging youth for chasing happiness and making life changes more often than most of us change the oil in our cars, perhaps we should consider them brave, resilient and adaptable.

TIPS AND TAKEAWAYS

- Model patience and loyalty in your own personal and professional life
- Share coping skills you find useful in times of stress
- Reframe your opinions to be more positive
- Check your own beliefs and be careful not to impose them on others
- Be the bigger person—show humility, vulnerability and empathy
- Be curious
- Consider your office environment—is it calming or distracting?

MYTH 2:

Youth are Addicted to Technology and Social Media

There are two sides to every coin. The use of technology is no different. It has the power to enlighten us, connect us and empower us. If used in excess, it can also wear us down. As technology continues to play a larger and larger role in our lives, we all have moments when we lose our balance. Because elders can remember a time before the global tech takeover, we may have a greater affinity for the real world and a higher value for face-to-face interactions.

Gen Z, who were born in the smartphone era, generally navigate the real and virtual worlds with ease, but tend to prefer the efficiency technology offers. What appears to be an addiction to instant gratification, may in fact be an aversion to the slow-moving pace of the real world.

THE MYTH: YOUTH ARE ADDICTED TO TECHNOLOGY AND SOCIAL MEDIA.

Last weekend, a friend and I visited a small mountain town in South Africa. On our second day, we decided to go for a hike. It was summer time in South Africa and the sun's warm rays cut through the towering trees, creating a luscious, natural beauty. After a few hours of walking through the woods, my friend and I came upon a waterfall. It was amazing! The powerful sound of the waterfall rushing, the greenery of the enchanted forest—it blew us away.

We rushed to the water to swim, wondering how we could get underneath the waterfall and feel the power of nature. It was invigorating!

As we stood in the water, we noticed two young people sharing the scene with us. One, a girl, had her back to the waterfall while her companion took pictures of her against this gorgeous backdrop. That was natural. I took pictures as well. However, for the entire hour that my friend and I swam, the girl continued taking selfies. It wasn't about the beauty of the waterfall. It was *her* beauty against an interesting backdrop. She was so focused on her next Instagram post that she was missing the entire moment.

To her credit, she had made an effort to get out in nature. Like us, she had hiked for hours to arrive at this oasis. The interesting duality of the situation is that while my friend and I were happy to put away our phones, the girl was using her phone to share her experience. This is where our two generations collide. We were immersing ourselves in nature. She was recording it. Self versus selfie.

We felt sorry for her lack of presence in this moment. Then it occurred to me that this *was* her way of being present. It bothered us that she spent the entire time on her mobile. It didn't bother her. She simply had different values, a different way of sharing and experiencing the moment.

Today's youth utilize technology in almost every aspect of their daily lives. Unlike millennials, who knew a world before the smartphone, Generation Z was born into it—many of them receiving their own cell phone by the age of ten. In this digital world, millennials and Gen Z have even created an entire genre of new, online careers—YouTube stars, content creators, gamers, and influencers are amongst the highest-grossing professionals these days. The top earner for 2019? An eight-year-old named Ryan Kaji, who creates videos in which he rates toys. His channel, *Ryan's World*, earned twenty-six million USD.[11] Tiktok, a relatively new social media app where people can create short music videos, exploded in 2019

---

11   "This eight-year-old remains YouTube's highest-earner, taking home $26 million in 2019," (Vicky McKeever, June 26, 2020), https://www.cnbc.com/2019/12/20/ryan-kaji-remains-youtubes-highest- earner-making-26-million-in-2019.html.

and its top earner, Addison Rae, earned five million USD in 12 months.[12]

Most high-profile celebrities utilize Instagram and Tik Tok to promote their brand, sell their products and reach a wider audience. Social media seems to be the key to gaining the attention—and the dollars—of the youth. Even former presidents and other high-ranking politicians have Twitter accounts, a platform that allows them to share their views and encourage youth to vote.

Gen Z is the first generation to grow up having unlimited access to knowledge and news in the palm of their hands. They are so inundated by a constant stream of information that their attention spans are becoming increasingly short, and harder to attract.

The term "snack media" was coined as a descriptor for how Gen Z consumes media—referring to short articles, podcasts and videos that share quick messages and can be digested while multitasking.[13] Everything needs to happen in seconds, not minutes or hours.

---

12   "TikTok's Highest-Earning Star Is Addison Rae, Who Takes Home $5 Million per Year (Report)," (Todd Spangler, August 6, 2020), https://variety.com/2020/digital/news/tiktok-highest-earning-stars-addison-rae-charli-damelio-1234727502/

13   "Generation Z – A Flux Trends Report," (Flux Trends, June 2020), https://www.fluxtrends.com/downloads/generation-z-flux-trends-report/.

Access to technology has become so invasive, there is now a term psychologists use for being without your phone—nomophobia.[14]

There are rehabilitation centers that treat those addicted to their mobile phones.

An American Addiction Center Resource compares mobile addictions to gambling and shopping compulsions, and describes treatment options such as one-on-one therapy, cognitive behavioral therapy and motivational interviewing.[15] You could even attend a support group such as Internet and Tech Addiction Anonymous (ITAA), which offers a twelve-step program similar to Alcoholics Anonymous or Narcotics Anonymous.

Houston, we have a problem.

This seems like an opportune moment to discuss the rising rates of depression and anxiety in millennials and Generation Z. Various studies have been done linking anxiety and depression

---

14   "Smartphone Addiction," (Lawrence Robinson, Melinda Smith, M.A., and Jeanne Segal, Ph.D., September 2020), https://www. helpguide.org/articles/addictions/smartphone-addiction.htm.

15   "Self-Treatment for Cell Phone Addiction," (PsychGuides. com), https://www.psychguides.com/behavioral-disorders/smart-phone-addiction/.

with high smartphone usage, and the strong correlation relates to several factors.[16]

1. Social comparison.

2. Increased stress and burnout due to unclear boundaries between work and home.

3. Lack of focus/increasing rates of ADHD due to the constant flow of, and access to, information and entertainment.

4. Disruptive sleep patterns.

5. Increasing levels of narcissism and self-absorption.

WHAT LIES BENEATH THE SURFACE

For those of us in older generations, our tribe consisted of our immediate family, our classmates and our community.

We were limited to a very small circle of friends and acquaintances based mostly on convenient geography. If you were lucky, you might have found a few really good friends who shared similar interests as you. However, if you were one of those unfortunate kids who didn't quite fit the mould, finding a friend may have proved a challenge. Maybe you were the outcast or the loner. Maybe this loneliness wasn't always your choice.

---

16   "Adolescent mental health," (World Health Organization, September 28, 2020), https://www.who.int/news-room/fact-sheets/detail/adolescent-mental-health.

One of the benefits of technology is that it has widened the scope of the tribe. No matter what your interests are, you will likely find similar people on the internet. If you are suffering from an illness or have an issue, you will likely find support from people who have survived similar circumstances and can impart some wisdom and advice. Even if you are the quirky kid who doesn't quite fit in with the peer group in your tiny, isolated town, chances are, you can find a kindred spirit and a sense of connection on the internet.

Not only are young people finding friendship and love online, they are also using the space to learn from each other. YouTube has become society's DIY bible. You can learn absolutely anything—from how to take a stunning photograph, to how to change the oil in your car, to how to write an attention-grabbing resume. Youth have access to a breadth of knowledge like no other generation before them and this knowledge has spilled over into their political savvy as well. I grew up with World Book Britannica, the primary resource if you had a question. I also could ask my teachers, my friends or my parents. Now young people enjoy learning that has no boundaries. These limitless boundaries include the possibility of gathering tribes of like minded people who not only benefit from each other's knowledge, but imagine the possibilities of change.

Youth today boast an incredible awareness of politics, global conflicts, human rights violations and environmental crises. Using the internet, they easily educate themselves, find others with a shared passion, brainstorm solutions and create tangible action plans. As a result, even those who are too young to vote, feel inspired to rise up, gather and make change.

In an article written for *The Guardian*, reporter Simon Tisdall said, "Thanks to social media, the ubiquity of English as a common tongue, and the internet's globalisation and democratisation of information, younger people from all backgrounds and locations are more open to alternative life choices, more attuned to "universal" rights and norms such as free speech or a living wage – and less prepared to accept their denial."[17]

Gen Z is a generation of youth who believe their higher purpose is to fix the world they've inherited. They are critical thinkers, who are creating solutions on a global scale. Their birth into technology is what has primed them for success.

WHAT DOES THIS MEAN?

The truth is, we all spend too much time on our mobiles. We enjoy the freedom our phones allow us, the ability to manage our lives from anywhere in the world. The downside to this is a constant exposure to notifications and news. We all become overwhelmed by the barrage of information, much of it depressing and demotivating. On top of that, tech platforms

---

17   "About 41% of the global population are under 24. And they're angry…," (Simon Tisdall, October 26, 2019), https://www. theguardian.com/world/2019/oct/26/young-people-predisposed-shake-up-established- order-protest.

know how much we depend on our mobiles and they exploit it, keeping us addicted.

Young people are suffering from mental health issues in greater numbers than we have ever seen. The rates of anxiety, depression, sleep-deprivation and suicide are off the charts. People, while being globally connected like never before in history, are also the loneliest they have ever been, suffering from a lack of deep, meaningful connection.

Gen Z are not unaware of the duality of technology. In fact, we can thank them for "outing" mental health. Mental health has come out of the closet and into the mainstream. We have all been suffering, but Gen Z wants to talk about it. The irony of it all is, they are using social media as their platform for discussion. The very thing that harms them is the thing they turn to for spreading the message.

Elders need to remind young people of the importance of switching off in order to replenish. Every once in a while, we need to tune out and log off to block out the noise. We also need to remind them to balance the digital and real world. There is no denying that technology is incredibly useful, but it should not be our only resource and should not replace authentic human connection.

Young people tend to be conflict averse, using email and text to have difficult conversations—even in the workplace. They lack the interpersonal skills to tactfully manage emotions that boil when opinions clash. Communication is very different for them and may require a level of compromise from us. In my house, my daughters often text me when they have a problem or something sensitive to share. While I encourage them to reach out to me whenever they need to, and would certainly prefer a face-to-face conversation, I would rather have a digital conversation than no conversation at all.

AN ASIDE FOR BUSINESS OWNERS...

Gen Z is a force to be reckoned with. They are our present and future market and they care about more than simple consumerism. They hold enormous commercial power and they use this power to support brands that align with their values. Youth are brand loyal and feel that companies have a responsibility to contribute to society in meaningful ways. "Generation Z expects brands to add value to the world. They don't want to buy a logo, they want to buy from someone who stands for something."[18]

Technology is used as a research tool for brand investigation. For Gen Z, advertising alone doesn't work. This generation prefers online reviews and places a weighty value on word of mouth.[9] Along with reviews, they will consult friends, family and social media influencers to seek out specific products and brands. What are their friends buying? What products are

---

18   "Generation Z – A Flux Trends Report," (Flux Trends, June 2020), https://www.fluxtrends.com/downloads/generation-z-flux-trends-report/.

their favorite online personalities using? "Keep Gen Z's phone dependence at the forefront of everything companies do to attract and retain customers."[19]

Gen Z is a force to be reckoned with.

Designing advertisements that focus on images, rather than text will attract more attention, and using short form videos to engage Gen Z on a personal level is equally effective. Furthermore, if you use these videos and images to tell a story that explains the *why* behind your brand (i.e. your company leaves a small carbon footprint, or you are selling a healthy and vibrant lifestyle) your appeal will increase.

However, if you are not true to your word, young people will call you out. In the past, a company's greatest fear was becoming irrelevant. Now, they need to deal with cancel culture. You are not irrelevant. You are dead.

It's not just clients who are socially aware, employee activism is on the rise. These Gen Z social justice warriors are now old enough to work for you and are holding their own employers accountable—even at the risk of their own careers. If your

---

19   "Zconomy: How Gen Z Will Change the Future of Business and What to Do About It," (Dorsey, Jason, 2020.) Harper Business; Illustrated edition.

company claims to hold certain values and your actions contradict that, you can expect an internal breach.

Collaboration is your lifeline. You need to work *with* young people. They want to work *with* you and they want to work *for* you, but their caveat is, they want you to care.

There is a sub**section** of Gen Z that I like to call "Gen Hustle." These young people are action-oriented and have been referred to as "go getters going their own way." They are turning their passions into businesses and using their businesses to serve the world in a positive way, while earning a profit. While Gen Hustle wants to do things their own way, they recognize the need for mentorship. They want brands and big businesses to help them scale. Essentially, they need guidance from the elders.

Take for example, the South African company Grumpy Snacks, which was co-founded by Cait Black. Cait, who self-admittedly gets a little grumpy when she's hungry, was looking for a healthy, vegan food that was convenient.

As a result, she created Grumpy Snacks, a cleverly branded, delicious snack of roasted chickpeas. Grumpy Snacks was quickly noticed by a South African airline called Lift, who was in search of cool, local artisanal brands to support. This collaboration has elevated Grumpy Snacks to a level which far exceeded Cait's hopes and dreams. She is now sharing a snack that's good for your health and for the environment on a national scale.

BRANDS WHO WALK THE WALK: GETTING BEHIND YOUR VALUES

Miki Agrawal, a Canadian entrepreneur, speaker and author prides herself on using "creativity and disruptive innovation to challenge the status quo and change culture." As the founder and CEO of multiple businesses (Wild, Tushy and THINX— which have grossed over $200 million), she has intentionally allocated both time and money to helping others. Miki has written two books (Do Cool Sh*t and Disrupt-Her) which are meant to guide youth in making effective change. She has organized a mentoring program that coaches young entrepreneurs who are venturing into their own startups. She has also used profit from her company, THINX, to help over 100,000 girls in Uganda go to school. A Generation Xer, Miki Agrawal has made a concerted effort to engage and support those who are up-and-coming in this world.

American ice cream conglomerate Ben and Jerry's made a public statement in 2020 after weeks of intense racial protesting throughout the country and the government's lack of response to the national upset. After declaring that their company has never been one to shy away from the political battlefield, co-founder Ben Cohen and his company released a line of politically charged ice cream flavors including White Macadamia Nut Privilege, Orange Impeachment, Apple Pie Anarchy and Strawberry Supremacy Sorbet.

The Levi's jean brand is notorious for publicly standing up for issues from gun control to voting policy. In the spring of 2021, CEO and president, Chip Bergh, made a television appearance on CNN calling out new American voting measures as restrictive and racist. In response to these policies, he declared that Levi's would support legislation to change these laws and would be donating money to non-profit organizations who ensure fair and equal access to the polls.

TIPS AND TAKEAWAYS

- We are all addicted to technology but the question is to what extent?

- Young people are using technology to coordinate movements for global change

- Elders need to remind young people to create balance between the digital world and the real world

- Brands and businesses need to collaborate with youth

- Be authentic or be cancelled

MYTH 3:

Youth are Entitled

The hallmark of a millennial was their entitlement—having been "the boss" from day one. They were brought up by parents who overcompensated for their own lack of parental nurturing with helicopter parenting—wrapping kids in a cotton wool of self confidence. I tend to wonder if this overconfidence is a compensation as well. I suspect that millennials suffer from massive insecurity and need to have their path mapped out in order to see all the twists and turns. Being wrapped in cotton wool has robbed millennials of the ability to manage life's uncertainties.

Generation Z does not appear to hold this same anxiety. Their worries are at a higher level. They are concerned about the environment, the government, the injustice they see in the world.

Gen Z tends to get lumped in with the millennials, who wanted gold stars for "adulting." In this chapter, I'd like to suggest that what appears to be entitlement is not only the result of the way millennials were parented, but is a generational bug that was fixed in the Gen Z software upgrade.

MYTH: YOUTH ARE ENTITLED

Adulting:

Noun: the practice of behaving in a way characteristic of a responsible adult, especially the accomplishment of mundane but necessary tasks.

Young people believe they should be congratulated for their "achievements" and amongst these "achievements" they list tasks such as laundry, cooking, grocery shopping, paying bills, and showing up for work on time. They complain that the very jobs that pay for said groceries are interfering with their social lives, their hobbies and their family time. Don't they know that adults have been performing these duties, without complaint, for centuries? These are not achievements. They are daily necessities required by most humans on the planet.

I suppose we shouldn't be surprised by their attitude and need for constant recognition. These are the same people who were given everything as children. They had the best toys, the fanciest vacations, played for the best teams, and attended the most prestigious schools. If they forgot their lunch, their mom would deliver it to school for them. If they didn't do their homework, their father would write a note explaining why, saving them from the consequences. If they received a poor grade, their parents would meet with the teacher and ask why he or she wasn't supporting their child in class. If they had a disagreement on the playground, their folks would wonder what the other child did to provoke it and contact their parents. Children were never asked to do chores or get a job. They were hardly left alone or out of sight. They were always consulted about their feelings and were encouraged to follow their passions. Every single one of them was special.

WHAT LIES BENEATH THE SURFACE

At the risk of sounding like a broken record, I'd like to remind you that we created this issue. Many young elders, such as myself, grew up with parents who were unavailable— emotionally or physically. In many households, both parents worked full-time jobs in order to make ends meet, thus leaving their children to fend for themselves. Our hardworking parents were conservative with money and they let us know. *"Do you think money grows on trees?" "We're broke."* As children, many of us were inundated with constant messages of a looming financial crisis, thus we were forced to go without. Luckily, most of us did not have to go without food or shelter, but we certainly went without the coolest shoes, the nicest clothes and fancy vacations. We may not have been spoiled, but we certainly learned the value of money and the concept of money being finite.

> We created this issue.

When we grew up and became parents ourselves, we vowed to go the extra mile and "provide" for our children. We provided an overabundance of love, attention, support and material items. Our children would never hear the statement *"we're broke"* and feel the fear and guilt of that reality. Instead, we would provide by buying on credit and feel proud that our children had everything they needed to set themselves up for success.

Our children were shielded from our financial concerns and material items seemed to appear easily—almost from thin air. *"Your wish is my command."* Therefore, millennials, especially, did not learn the value of money. They simply asked and were promptly rewarded. They did not know how hard their parents worked, how precariously close their parents may have been creeping toward financial collapse in order to provide for their children.

Social media certainly contributed to this cocktail as parents were constantly aware of what others were providing for their children: vacations, experiences, activities. Comparison is a breeding ground for competition. If you want your child to make the most prestigious sports team, then they need the personal training and the nutritionist that will make them a competitive athlete. If you want your child to be accepted into the best schools, then they will need to take violin lessons, get language tutoring and all the things the other children are doing. Many times, the children didn't even ask for these extras, but were pressured and pushed by eager parents who may have been denied similar luxuries and support in their own childhood.

When it comes to "adulting", one online article suggests that youth have been raised by parents who were hyper-focused on productivity, using it as a measuring stick for self-worth.[20] *How hard did you work today? How much multitasking are you capable of? How much sleep are you lacking?* Exhaustion, stress and being busy were worn as badges of honor. As a result, millennials and, perhaps Gen Z, have grown to live their lives in terms of to-do lists—robbing them of the opportunity to experience joy.

These impossibly high standards seem to have created an overwhelming anxiety, which stunned and paralyzed millennials. Perhaps they were not entitled, but simply could not carry the weight of the expectation society placed on them (or that they placed upon themselves). They had lofty ambitions and big dreams, but just couldn't transfer those ideas into action.

In regards to this particular myth, I suggest that it may be limited to the millennial generation. Generation Z appears to have a much more grounded set of values and expectations when it comes to money and opportunities. An article written in the *Huffington Post* suggests one reason for this is that most children in Gen Z are being raised by parents who grew up

---

20   "How Millennials Became The Burnout Generation," (Anne Helen Petersen, January 5, 2019), https://www.buzzfeednews.com/article/annehelenpetersen/millennials-burnout-generation-debt-work.

in Generation X and witnessed the child-rearing mistakes of those who came before them.[21] Their number one parenting goal was not to raise another generation of millennials—who were considered to be unmotivated, uninspired and entitled.

Additionally, those in Gen Z were heavily affected by the Great Recession, the economic bust of 2008. Many in Gen Z watched their parents lose their jobs and their homes. As a result of this perspective-changing event, this group of youth generally place priority on saving, many of them attempting to graduate college with as little debt as possible. They love a bargain and tend to be frugal with their spending.

In terms of wanting more, with less, I might suggest that both the millennials and Gen Z *do* have more, with less. More student debt, and less opportunity to own their own home. More pollution, with less political and economic stability. They have, essentially, been handed the global problems we have created, with the expectation that the youth will solve the issues. They are our greatest hope for a better world, and this carries the enormous weight of responsibility. The good news is, I believe they can do it. So, yes, we may make fun of them for their achievements in adulting. Meanwhile, we mustn't forget to thank them for the outstanding efforts they are making in the realms of political, social and environmental change.

---

21 "There's A Big Difference Between Millennials And Generation Z," (Casey Bond, August 7, 2020), https://www.huffpost.com/entry/millennials-gen-z-differences_1_5f2b87f6c5b6e96a22adc439.

WHAT DOES THIS MEAN?

We need to begin by taking ownership of the problem. Young people are entitled because we let them be that way. This dependency upon others to problem solve and create opportunity began in early childhood when parents spent too much time "protecting" their children from risk. Anne Helen Petersen reminds us that parents have notoriously reminded children not to "play on dangerous playground structures, go out without a cellphone, or drive without an adult in the car." We have micromanaged our children into helplessness.

In order to reverse this mindset or to prevent it from occurring in future generations, it is imperative that we allow our youth the necessary space to explore and to make mistakes. We need to encourage them to take risks and know, undoubtedly, that the expectation is never for perfection, but for improvement. We don't mind if they fail in the pursuit of learning.

It has been suggested that this compulsive striving for perfection is what has paralyzed millennials, rendering them incapable of action—even robbing them of opportunities for joy and memory making. As elders, we should make an effort to model a healthy balance between work and play, seriousness and silliness. Yes, there are times to take ourselves seriously, to concentrate on important tasks, and to check things off our lists. It is equally important to prioritize and drop tasks that prohibit us from experiencing the happiness life can offer. This balance is not irresponsible. It is necessary. Taking time away from work recharges your batteries so that you may continue to be productive and innovative, performing to the best of your ability.

My last piece of advice for elders who wish to guide their tribe is that we need to be mindful of our own biases and opinions. It's natural for the elder generations to misunderstand youth— their priorities, their choices, their passions, their ideas. It's also natural to feel somewhat offended when youth don't buy into things we believe work well, or appreciate the battles we fought to gain advantages. Their disinterest isn't personal. They are simply carving their own path, just as we did before them.

When relationships suffer from a level of disconnect, it becomes very easy to illuminate differences and annoyances. They are disloyal. They lack patience. They are addicted to technology. They are entitled. We slip into negativity, frustration and even resentment. The "us and them" mentality is human nature, after all. While it's perfectly understandable to acknowledge societal differences with those who succeed us, we must be cautious not to alienate youth with our heavy-handed opinions. They are simply doing what they feel is right, just, interesting and efficient and it's okay if they don't seek our stamp of approval.

I encourage you to remember the advances we have made *because* of our youth, not despite them. Technology has improved because of youthful innovation. Steve Jobs created the first Macintosh computer in his father's garage. Mark Zuckerberg invented Facebook in his university dorm room. Not everyone understood these groundbreaking inventions immediately. Like anything else, they fought skepticism while mastering their craft and it took a while for the general public to catch on. We admire the brilliance of these mavericks, now, because we have the gift of time and retrospect.

Instead of criticizing young people, we should be praising them for being brave, being imaginative, for going against the grain and following their passions. They provide fresh eyes and encourage us to view things from a different perspective. While I may not be able to convince you to let go of your preconceived notions and opinions (which are most likely backed by some experience), I hope I can encourage you to retain some balance. There are two sides to every coin and nothing is entirely negative. Youth have exponentially more to offer than we give them credit for. One of the most valuable traits a young elder can have is an open mind. It will always serve you well and will open space for meaningful connection.

TIPS AND TAKEAWAYS

- Provide space for risk taking and mistake-making—perfection is never the expectation
- Encourage proper prioritization and a healthy work-life balance
- Keep negative opinions to yourself and choose to focus on positive contributions

SECTION 3:

HOW DID WE GET HERE?

CHAPTER SEVEN
THE PARTICIPATION MEDAL GENERATION

A few years ago, my daughter received an award for sports at school. At the time, my daughter didn't play any sports. The only conceivable way that she could have received an award was by attending a netball (a sport similar to basketball) practice *once* because she had a social engagement afterwards with a friend who was on the team. Rather than sitting and waiting, she may have decided to bounce a ball around. Though it was the lowest form of participation possible, she was rewarded for her "efforts."

Many of us look at youth, remark on their sensitive nature, lack of motivation and sense of entitlement and ask, *"How did we get here?"* We worry that the children we are raising lack the grit, wisdom and work ethic necessary to become the next generation of leaders.

Read that last sentence again—the children *we are raising...*

I like to think of this issue as a big, old tree. We look at the branches, twisted and fragile, worried that they may break at any moment. What we fail to investigate are the roots of the tree. Are they strong? Well-grounded? Reliable? The branches are our youth, the obvious point of reference to worry about because they are the easiest to see. Yes, a branch may break, but if the roots are unsteady, the entire tree will come crashing down. We are the roots. Those who came before, those who raised children and those who mentored. A tree doesn't grow from top down, it grows from the roots up. If the roots fail, the entire organism doesn't stand a chance.

Basically what I'm saying is, before we look at the problems of youth, we need to look at ourselves.

These days, children are rewarded and praised simply for existing. We encourage *"Good job"* and *"Well done"* or *"You're incredible"* as easily as we breathe in the air around us. We hand out ribbons, medals and trophies to all participants, so their feelings don't get hurt. We tell our children how much we love them, how important they are, how smart they seem and how beautiful they look multiple times per day. As a result, we have raised children who do not need to *earn* accolades, they simply need to show up.

How does this complimentary culture affect those children who *are* working hard and *are* making astounding achievements? Are they aware that their contributions and efforts are extraordinary, or do they feel lumped in with those who put forth the bare minimum effort? What motivates children to work hard, considering they will be praised regardless of their grit or lack thereof? Do children differentiate those with talent and those without? What happens to these children when they grow up and join the workforce?

I suppose the other side of the coin is that recognizing all children creates inclusivity, worthiness and belonging. No one is left out. No one is unseen. It combats the culture of "to each his own" and swings to the other end of the spectrum. I'm not entirely sure which approach does the most damage or good.

In recent years, one of the primary complaints from employers is that millennial and Gen Z employees require constant praise for just showing up and have an insatiable need for instant feedback. They feel deserving of a high five or an appreciative nod simply for showing up. They complain when they aren't constantly validated, feeling unseen or ignored. For employers born in earlier generations, this need for constant nurturing and unearned praise can seem exhausting, even ridiculous. We complain about the unmotivated, disloyal, needy and entitled youth, but I would like to remind you that we created this dynamic. We raised these children. These branches are from our trees.

HOW DID WE GET HERE?

If you are a baby boomer, you were probably raised by a father who came home from work, turned on the television, grabbed the newspaper and a beer. He was tired after a long day and was not to be disturbed. Once in a while, he may make an acknowledging grunt in your direction, and a pat on the head was about as close to physical connection as it got. Most likely, you spent your entire childhood—and perhaps your entire life—hoping to please your father, to catch his attention and earn a word of praise. Some of you never received it. If you were one of the lucky few whose father happened to mention he was proud of you, that rare praise inspired a delicious dopamine hit that turned us into achievement chasers, seeking our next fix.

Baby boomers were raised by fathers who were taught that showing emotion or affection was feminine and a sign of weakness. As a result, children were left with a feeling of never living up to expectations, or they suffered from a lack of meaningful connection with one of their idols.

If you are from Generation X, you may have been raised on autopilot, with huge chunks of unsupervised time in the cockpit. While you probably grew up to become self-sufficient, you may have missed the opportunity to spend time with the adults who were supposed to be raising you, who probably wished they *could* raise you, but were confined by the societal norm of working parents. Parents were not around to show affection, to observe adventures and praise growth, and when they arrived home at the end of a busy day, they were simply exhausted. Too tired to connect. Families may have eaten dinner together, but they were going through the motions, vacant of emotion. Kids can appreciate the need to pay the bills but on the other side, they feel abandoned. This becomes a wound they carry through to adulthood, which plays out both in the workplace and in relationships.

These parental deficiencies are no one's fault. They are simply a result of societal demands and expectations. When children grow up and become parents themselves, their style of connection, affection and communication is often a direct result of how they were raised. How many times have you heard someone vow, *"My kids will never experience that"*? Baby boomers and Generation Xers have swung to the opposite end of the spectrum. Remembering their days of cold, unapproachable and unavailable parents, they consciously decided to do differently. They vowed to be kind, affectionate, connected and present. Perhaps their approach was slightly over exaggerated.

You may be familiar with the term "Helicopter Parent"—that mother or father who micromanages every aspect of their children's lives. We go to extreme lengths to protect their children from perceived danger. We have bubbled-wrapped our children, so as to protect them from failure. We make excuses or demand a second chance. We have essentially overmanaged our children to the point that they do not know how to manage themselves. We have not allowed our children to think for themselves, to advocate for their own needs, or to fail and overcome adversity.

In addition, we have stopped expecting our children to contribute with acts of service to lighten the load. Most of us born in earlier generations were expected to perform household chores. Perhaps you were asked to cut the lawn, to do your laundry, or to babysit your siblings. I was expected to work at the family business from a very young age—giving up my freedom to learn the ropes and help the family.

We felt overburdened by responsibility and while we didn't love it, we took one for the team. By not asking youth to contribute, we rob them of the opportunity to be a team player and, instead, raise children who may become helpless and entitled.

WHAT DOES THIS MEAN?

Let's face it—everyone likes to be validated and recognized when they feel they have achieved something, or have put forth an impressive effort. Appreciation can be connected to our basic human need for belonging. We all want to be seen. We all want to be heard. While validation and praise are a necessary ingredient for successful mentoring and parenting, it should be the cherry on top of the ice cream sundae—not the ice cream.

When praise becomes the bulk of our communication, it becomes meaningless and can actually do more harm than good. As young elders, we have so much more to offer—encouragement, support, honest feedback, accountability and advice. This type of communication is not only authentic, but will cultivate a space for growth. When we continually tell our youth that they are "perfect" and everything they do is "amazing", this discounts any motivation to evolve and do better. If you are already perfect, where do you go from there?

We can't chastise our youth for being unmotivated while simultaneously praising their excellence.

Elders need to lead by example. Our actions speak the loudest. Gen Z is a values-driven generation and they want to establish their own set of values and purpose. Instead of responding to their questions and demands with the typical parenting defense, "*Because I said so!*", we should take the time to guide. We can help youth understand the *why* behind our choices so that they can formulate their own *why*. We need to normalize imperfection and explain the reasons for our decisions—even when they don't turn out as we had planned. We may not always be amazing, but we are always learning.

> Elders need to lead by example.

> "A mistake that makes you humble is better than an achievement that makes you arrogant."
> ANONYMOUS

TIPS AND TAKEAWAYS

- The journey is more important than the result
- Encourage your kids to explore as many things as possible—it's through exploration that they uncover their passions
- Encourage youth to fail and to persevere
- Create quality time with your kids and allocate emotional bandwidth
- Find reasons to connect with them, be intentional—meal times and car rides are opportunities to discuss something of value
- Screen time is a tradable commodity

CHAPTER EIGHT
ANXIETY NATION

TECHNOLOGY AND MENTAL HEALTH

When was the last time you went to bed tired, but plagued by a brain that won't turn off? Many of us suffer from ruminating thoughts that keep us awake at night. After finally falling asleep, we wake up, only to discover that the negative thoughts are still there. We are stuck in a thought loop. Our media feed works in exactly the same way—with our reality being served to us and reinforced by our previous internet searches. It's easy to get stuck in a negative loop.

Young people suffer from hyperconnectivity—they are always "on" and always multitasking while being overwhelmed by information. It's great for productivity, but the other side of the coin is that this massive exposure to screen time messes with their sleep and their mental health. They become locked in a holding pattern of negativity and memes. Your media feed becomes your reality, with algorithms serving you more of what you are already looking at, reinforcing your version of "truth." In this information loop, it becomes easy to lose perspective.

Even though technology is a valuable tool for connecting us to like-minded people and causes, streaming apps suck us into a vortex of self-isolation. People don't gather to watch television together any more. Young people are watching their devices in their rooms, with no need to move unless they are hungry, need to go to the bathroom or to retrieve a delivery at the door. The irony of virtual connection is that it has created a culture of aloneness.

Data gathered in early 2020 declares that up to 20% of the global youth population suffer from a mental health disorder.[22] Your first reaction to that statistic is to blame Covid, and you're not wrong. Covid-19 has amplified the mental health crisis on a worldwide scale—financial difficulties, isolation, illness and relationship stresses have put most of us in a vulnerable and delicate state. What is shocking to me, however, are the pre-Covid numbers, which show that mental health issues were skyrocketing in our youth even before the pandemic.

---

22   "Mental Health," (The World Bank, April 2020), https://www.worldbank.org/en/topic/mental-health.

In 2017, 792 million young adults worldwide identified themselves as having a mental health disorder.[23] That's approximately 10% of the youth population on a global scale. Does anyone else find that statistic astounding?

> The irony of virtual connection is that it has created a culture of aloneness.

It means that one in ten born in Gen Z suffer from depression, anxiety and panic disorders—amongst other diagnoses. To be clear, these statistics represent disorders that have been formally diagnosed. The numbers do not include youth who suffer from a lesser degree of worry, melancholy and/or hopelessness, nor does it account for those who are undiagnosed and untreated.

Generation Z worries about the environment, political rights, human rights, going to college, paying for college, student debt, getting a job that contributes to society, diversity, inclusion, saving money for the future, and, and, and... While millennials earned a reputation for being egocentric and lacking ambition or foresight, it seems Generation Z has swung in the opposite direction entirely. They are so consumed with living up to their potential, building a stable future and global issues, that they have forgotten how to lighten up and relax.

---

23   "Mental Health," (Hannah Ritchie and Max Roser, April 2018), https://ourworldindata.org/mental-health.

Authors and researchers Jason R. Dorsey and Denise Villa acknowledge this epidemic of anxiety amongst our youth and ask how could this *not* happen?[24] In their formative years, Generation Z has had a front-row seat to more strife than many of us witness in a lifetime. They were born into a world of divisive politics, fake news, cancel culture and polarization. They have seen gay marriage legalized. They have heard news or hold firsthand experiences of school shootings and extreme violence at concerts and other public events. They are sensitive to climate change and environmental issues. They have seen women rising up against discrimination and unwanted sexual advances and know that the world is still unsafe for some of us. They watch or attend racial justice rallies. Because of the immersive virtual reality they live in, Gen Z is able to band together to fight against these injustices but that immersive culture is also an anxiety superfood, creating a hyper-awareness of negativity in the world.

Generation Z has, most likely, experienced a high level of stress in their own homes as well—being raised by parents who were affected by the 2008 economic recession. Those same parents are now caught in a financial crisis of competing priorities— still recovering from prior loss of income, paying off their own enormous debts while trying to plan for the future. According to Dorsey and Villa, Generation Z has a fiscal awareness

---

24   "Zconomy: How Gen Z Will Change the Future of Business and What to Do About It," (Dorsey, Jason, 2020.) Harper Business; Illustrated edition.

and desire for practicality not seen since youth raised in the Great Depression of the 1930s. As a result of their own stress, many parents have been engaging their growing children in conversations about money since they were old enough to comprehend the topic.

Many have gone so far as to suggest that financial literacy (budgeting, investing and saving) be taught in our schools in an effort to better prepare young people for the future. While these are important life skills, one might say they are being taught from a place of fear—we don't want you to suffer like we have.

WHAT DOES THIS MEAN?

As elders—whether you are a parent or professional mentor—I believe our primary role in terms of supporting Generation Z's underlying anxiety is to initiate conversations and create a safe space, free of judgment, for youth to share their concerns with us. This may mean we offer explicit advice on how to cope with stress. It may also require us to have conversations about world events, politics, and tragedies, helping them digest all they have seen and heard. We should encourage Gen Z to take action—to be social justice warriors—if working to create change helps them feel empowered in a world that can be both unjust and scary.

While they fight for what's right, they must also remember that the responsibility to save the world does not lie solely on one person's back. Collaboration, support, determination and change is the responsibility of many. We can remind the youth that while they are fighting for what's right, they shouldn't let that battle be all-consuming. It may be perfectly understandable for Gen Z to worry about the future, but it's equally important for them to enjoy the present. Balance comes in work and play, virtual and real world connection. This is where we can help.

Elders can remind young people to get off of their devices and get into their bodies. Turn off their phones and step into nature. Our bodies manufacture all the depression-fighting chemicals naturally. All it takes is a little exercise, sunshine and fresh air to access them. We know that our bodies and minds are interconnected. When we move, we feel better, we think better. Dancing, breathwork, great sleep, healthy foods, and laughter—it all adds up to sustainable mental health.

It's also important to remind young people that not all change is immediate. Yes, we have seen spontaneous changes such as cancel culture and the GameStop stock market crunch — but a lot of change happens in small steps, rather than giant leaps. It's natural for there to be some tension when change is breaching, between the elder's natural default to preach patience and youth's need for instant gratification. In a fast-paced world, young people may find a level of dissatisfaction when the effects of their efforts are not instantaneous. In these moments, we can remind them that slow progress does not necessarily equate to failure.

Most importantly, whether they are creating a financial plan, organizing social justice rallies or creating awareness about global events, simply asking our youth, "How can I support you?" not only cultivates connection and acceptance, but may serve to reduce anxiety. Knowing that you are seen, heard, understood and supported decreases the feeling that one is fighting alone. It immediately places both the elder and the youth on the same team. If you are a financial whiz, offer to help with their college tuition plan, retirement savings, or monthly budget. If you are skilled with social media, offer to spearhead an online campaign for the cause they are passionate about. Getting involved cultivates trust and makes space for collaboration. It also creates opportunities for reciprocal mentoring.

One of our primary roles as elders is to broaden youth perspectives, but we can't forget that we also have a lot to learn. We can learn so much from young people and, in mentoring, often our perspectives shift and evolve too. It's said that one of the most effective ways to combat polarization is to broaden your own views. This is one area where we need to walk the walk, not just talk the talk. In this mentoring, though, it's important to remember that while we support and guide, youth will take the information we provide and want to process it in a way that's meaningful to them and relevant in their world. They will still do things their own way.

Lastly, elders need to engage in conversations about mental health. While both millennials and Gen Z have blown the lid off of previously-held stigmas, elders need to set aside our own preconceptions and reservations when it comes to talking about depression and anxiety. We need to cultivate an environment where it is perfectly acceptable to admit one is struggling and to ask for help—whether that admission be to a colleague, a leader, a friend or a family member. We should know the signs of distress and support young people by reacting with compassion and empathy.

TIPS AND TAKEAWAYS

- Encourage balance in every aspect of life: work/play, virtual world/real world, access to news/turning off your phone, being restful/moving your body

- Create a safe, non-judgmental space to have courageous conversations about anxiety, fear, world events and mental health

- Collaborate and engage in reciprocal mentoring

- Be aware of signs of mental health struggles and support youth with coping strategies

- Seek medical advice when necessary

SECTION 4:

WHAT DOES THE FUTURE LOOK LIKE?

PART 1

THE FUTURE OF WORK

"If [business is] not listening to the youth, they are not listening to their future competition, employees or customers."

WADIA AIT HAMZA

Head of the Global Shapers
of the World Economic Forum

CHAPTER NINE
THE FUTURE OF THINKING

"What got you here won't get you there."
MARSHALL GOLDSMITH

How much of your life is static, unchanging? How much of the world remains the same as it ever was? The last hundred years have been a constant evolution in almost every venue imaginable—workplace, technology, family structure, and environment. In the last decade, it seems that those changes are coming faster and more drastically. Society is in a constant state of violent breaching, new innovations, multiple disruptions and cultural shifts that are breaking through the status quo.

We are heading toward a new world, holding on to an old system. With constant change comes new challenges. We can no longer hang onto antiquated values and stagnant thinking.

The way we perceive and process the world around us needs a system upgrade. We need to change the way we think.

Traditionally, the purpose of school was to teach children how to conform to societal expectations so that they may become productive members of their community. Teachers were seen as the knower of all things—the ones who stand at the front of the classroom and teach you how to behave, how to cooperate and tell you which knowledge was important for you to remember. The goal was to learn, memorize and regurgitate facts, but not necessarily to exercise critical thinking.

> The way we perceive and process the world around us needs a system upgrade.

In those days, some of us were conformists and some of us, like myself, were rebels who wanted to ask deeper questions. Why? How? What if?

As the world changed, society began to recognize that the education system was not producing the type of citizens the world needed. The elders began to push the education system out of its comfort zone, forcing the establishment to realize the importance of deep understanding, and of creative and critical thinking.

In many modern classrooms, the teacher is no longer seen as the guru, but as a facilitator, asking big questions and encouraging students to work together to explore new ideas and skills. The classroom culture is no longer built upon bell curves and conformity, but has morphed into a more inclusive setting that celebrates diversity and individuality. The classroom has become a collaborative environment where all members of the team are necessary for success. This is a snapshot of the future workplace.

One of the upsides of the Covid-19 pandemic has been the opportunity for countries who were behind the curve in quality education to explore alternative means to learn. Technology has allowed students to teach themselves, to explore ideas that are meaningful and relevant to their generation. The way young people learn is changing.

In and out of school, elders are no longer teaching skills or facts. We are teaching a mindset. In the world of Google and YouTube, students no longer need to memorize meaningless facts so that they may spit them out in hopes of a perfect test score. They can simply ask Siri for the capital of Bangladesh or type into a search box to learn how to bake cupcakes. Instead, students are being encouraged to question, to investigate, to assess and to explore. We are teaching perseverance, resilience and collaboration—skills that have become increasingly valuable in today's workplace, which is constantly evolving and changing.

You may have heard the term design thinking. Some of us have always thought this way, so while it's not a new idea, it is now an adopted approach to learning in many schools. The goal of design thinking is to prepare students for the ever-changing nature of the world they will inherit. This way of thinking encourages a solution-based approach to solving problems and greatly affects the nature in which a young person processes information and makes decisions.

Design thinking coaches students to seek understanding, challenge assumptions and redefine problems. It advocates for intense questioning and collaboration in the quest to brainstorm possible solutions. It celebrates the ability to think outside of the box.

Humans generally fall prey to pattern-based thinking. When approaching a problem, we search the database of what we already know has worked or not worked in the past. We place enormous value on past experiences and accumulated knowledge. Pattern thinking limits our creativity and our ability to see a problem for what it truly is. Pattern thinking keeps us inside the box.

Design thinking is meant to push learners away from the familiar, in search of something better, greater, or more effective. It is a methodical approach to problem solving, which allows for a wider scope of possibilities. The steps to design thinking are as follows:

1. **Empathize** – Can we generate a holistic understanding of the issues people are facing?

2. **Define** – Investigate the problem and articulate the needs.

3. **Ideate** – Challenge assumptions and throw out past ways of doing things.

4. **Prototype** – Brainstorm possible solutions.

5. **Test** – Assess the success and sustainability of solutions.[25]

Why is this important? One of the principles of design thinking is to challenge assumptions and throw out past ways of doing things—an approach perfectly suited to next-generation thinking. It flat out says that we are supposed to ignore the way things have been done, and search for what is right, just, more efficient or better. Pay no attention to the road behind you. Look ahead and decide the best course of action based on your current observations and experiences. This is the lens through which Generation Z is looking at issues of equality, environment and government. This is the mindset that will create systemic change on scale.

WHAT DOES THIS MEAN?

Gen Z has been born and bred for collaboration. Many of them are naturally suited to team settings (virtual and physical), have the ability to communicate on multiple platforms simultaneously, and are hardwired for design thinking strategies which move organizations forward. They are "Generation We", rather than "Generation Me", which came before them. The ease and need for collaboration is

---

25   "5 Stages in the Design Thinking Process," (Rikke Friis Dam and Teo Yu Siang, January 2021), https://www.interaction-design.org/literature/article/5-stages-in-the-design-thinking-process.

embedded in their operating system, nurtured and encouraged by a new wave of education that focuses on problem solving more than the memorization of facts. Leaders in business and other organizations need to create environments that harness this collaborative approach in order to unleash this generation's magic.

Covid has played a huge role in ushering in the death of the office space as we know it, forcing employers to reconsider how teams organize themselves effectively while still preserving their workplace culture.

As some businesses decide to transition back to a shared working environment, a hybrid model seems to offer the best of both worlds—culture and flexibility.

Even before Covid-19, many of the most successful companies have chosen to flatten the hierarchy, giving more autonomy to teams within the organization. When leaders are open to unconventional ideas, it allows room for exploration, discovery and even failure. It creates space for creativity and innovation. By sticking to the status quo, the best possible outcome is incremental change. Companies looking to make radical advances need to embrace radical thinking.

Young people are looking to work for companies who share their values and who they believe have potential to make a difference in society and the world at large. They are seeking a professional outlet for their passions and want to contribute in a meaningful way.

The latter half of this book may challenge the way you see leadership. It may be uncomfortable. As the elder in my own company, Student Village, embracing a new leadership paradigm has been terrifying for me. From my own experience and what I'm seeing in the ever-changing world, I find myself asking what role the elders will continue to play in organizations that are becoming increasingly decentralized. Just like the teacher has become the facilitator, the destiny of an elder will follow suit.

TIPS AND TAKEAWAYS

- Design thinking is beginning to be introduced in schools, but is not globally pervasive yet
- Entry-level employees will be equipped with this approach to thinking
- The future workplace will become a hub of collaboration and culture
- Companies are beginning to flatten their hierarchical structure
- Constantly introduce new technology to improve collaboration and communication
- Stay connected with your teams and offer emotional support

CHAPTER TEN
THE FUTURE OF RECRUITING

Generation Z expects to contribute to society in a meaningful way and they wish to work for companies that allow them to do so. For this reason, Gen Z's wish list—when it comes to where they choose to work—may seem demanding but is not entirely unreasonable. Whereas salary may have been the primary determining factor in job seeking for older generations, it seems that Gen Z takes many other factors into consideration. Young people are essentially auditioning employers to be cast in their movie, searching for a match of values, purpose and passion.

Authors and researchers Dorsey and Villa investigated this very idea in their 2018 study of what Generation Z desires at work. The number one factor that matters to Gen Z is a great work environment.[26] Number two on the list was a flexible schedule, followed by on-the-job learning and talent development (62% of youth rate this as highly important).

The list also included traditional considerations such as health care benefits, retirement savings packages, paid time off, opportunities for career advancement and salary. Other, more untraditional requirements, were lifestyle-based perks such as a gym or yoga membership, discounts on internet service providers and tickets to special events.

Generation Z want to work at companies with a human-centric approach to their employees. These companies offer holistic packages that show employees they are valued and cared for. In researching companies where they may be applying to work, this generation will often consult YouTube, looking for examples of workplace culture. Do employees of the company enjoy their jobs? Do they feel like valued contributors? Does the company promote a work-life balance? Do employees feel they are allowed to be their authentic selves? While this may seem like a desire to be coddled, it's really more than that. Studies show that companies who care about their employees have a higher rate of retention and productivity. In fact, according to a Gallop research study, companies with highly engaged employees outperform by 147%.

---

26   "Zconomy: How Gen Z Will Change the Future of Business and What to Do About It," (Dorsey, Jason, 2020.) Harper Business; Illustrated edition.

> Generation Z want to work at companies with a human-centric approach to their employees.

As mentioned in the chapter on mental health, young people struggle with uncertainty—a challenge that was amplified by Covid-19. When applying for a job, youth want to see a clear career path outlined for them. Not only do they want to know how this job aligns with their hopes and dreams, but they also want to know how they will be supported and where there are opportunities to grow. They almost take a video game mentality to it—if I need to do this, then I will be rewarded with that. They want to know the rules of the game so that they can advance predictably.

Thanks to the internet and a new cultural acceptance for working from home, young people are not limited to jobs within their geographical area. They, quite literally, have the world as their oyster. For this reason, the competition for recruitment is steep and begins with the application process. Generation Z desires a mobile-friendly application—their go-to technology being a phone rather than a laptop or desktop computer. In addition, the application process must be short and easily navigated. In fact, 60% of youth say fifteen minutes is the maximum amount of time they are willing to spend completing an online application.[27]

In addition to the rapid application, young graduates expect a quick response from companies they apply at. The speed at which companies respond to graduates with offers will dramatically increase their success rate. This suggests that a winning approach to attract top young talent is a blend of certainty, fit and speed ... Did someone mention immediate gratification?!

WHAT DOES THIS MEAN FOR YOU?

As a business owner, if you want to remain relevant and attract young talent, you need to play the recruitment game by their rules. There is an abundance of motivated young people who are eager to join the workforce and if you want them to work for you, it will require you to throw away antiquated recruitment practices and change the way you do things.

First and most importantly, you must keep the smartphone at the center of everything that you do. Create a mobile-friendly application process that is short and sweet, advertise in popular forums with images that tell the story of your company, illustrate your values and encourage employee reviews and testimonials that Gen Z can research. Young people relate to

---

27   "Zconomy: How Gen Z Will Change the Future of Business and What to Do About It," (Dorsey, Jason, 2020.) Harper Business; Illustrated edition.

other young people, so take your rising stars and make them the heroes of your recruitment campaign.

Use social media wisely. If you are not in Gen Z's social feed, you don't exist. It's as simple as that. Statistics show that, when looking for a job, young people turn to their devices.

- 40% consult YouTube for top-rated companies and testimonials
- 37% consult Instagram
- 36% consult SnapChat[1]

One company who has used social media to its advantage is McDonalds. They have created "Snaplications" on SnapChat, that show ten-second videos of employees sharing why they love their job.[1] Viewers can then swipe to access a link to the application page. It's fun, engaging and easy to apply.

Knowing their reliance on social media, it's important to make sure everything you post aligns with the values you claim to uphold. Youth are always watching and they subscribe to a "cancel culture," which is essentially a public execution of individuals or brands which act or speak in a way that is either inappropriate or does not align with their stated values.

Secondly, you must remember that Gen Z is looking for much more than a salary offer. Taking a holistic, human-centered approach is the best way to entice young employees. Sell your culture. If you include the opportunity for mentorship, continuing education, leadership roles, collaboration, philanthropy and career advancement, then these will be your most effective selling points.

Creating a welcoming onboarding experience is an effective way to introduce an inclusive company culture. Gen Z, like most of us, have a strong desire to connect and belong. They want their workplace to feel like home, their colleagues to feel like family. They desire feedback, encouragement and support as they learn to grow and thrive within their new role.

Lastly, it's important to acknowledge that more than recruitment, *retention* should be the ultimate goal. Knowing how deeply Gen Z values purpose, passion, agency and freedom, it's probably no surprise that many young employees have a side hustle. *Their* end goal is to become their own boss by turning their passion into their career.

After investing time, money and energy to train our employees and integrate them into our teams, we want to keep them around! Understanding the importance of their side hustle is crucial to keeping youth happy. If we can promote employee passions, rather than deny or ignore them, it will create an appreciation which serves both parties. Supporting and even collaborating with employee side hustles has the potential to develop a mutually beneficial ecosystem; your employees will feel seen and valued, thereby increasing their loyalty to you and your company.

The unfortunate alternative is a low retention rate. Youth will leave your business as soon as their side hustle becomes remotely successful and financially stable, and you will find yourself with a revolving door of employees.

TIPS AND TAKEAWAYS

- They are casting you in *their* movie—do you represent their values and career aspirations?
- Your company's values should be well articulated on your website
- The faster your recruitment process, the better your chances are of attracting top talent
- Their social media feed is their reality so be a strong presence
- Keep the application process short and easy to navigate
- Offer a well-rounded, holistic employment package
- Personalize your onboarding experience
- Train them to be 'flexibility ready'
- Support their side hustle.

CHAPTER ELEVEN
THE FUTURE OF LEADERSHIP

*"Are there some areas where the more we push,
the more resistance we encounter—and when
we stop pushing, we find that we get what we
always wanted?"*
CONOR NEILL

Where have all the leaders gone? I have been thinking about this a lot lately. Ask yourself, "Who are three current leaders you can look up to?"

If you can think of one, you're doing well.

We used to look toward presidents, politicians, CEOs and activists to gather inspiration. The truth is, most young people no longer look up to these pillars of establishment. The younger generations have taken a good, hard look at the world around them—at the inefficient practices and at the corruption within power—and have decided they want nothing to do with it. They reject political leaders who sit in senate offices and on corporate boards, who know nothing about the experience of youth. They make decisions that are out of touch and out of date. Of course young people don't find inspiration there! They feel no connection or sense that they are understood. In fact, they feel relatively unseen.

As a result, rather than searching for an effective leader, youth are rejecting the idea of leaders altogether.

Once in a while, a renegade will emerge, a breath of fresh air that breaches the staleness. United States senator Alexandria Ocasio-Cortez (born in 1989) is a great example of the need to disrupt the establishment. Elected by a grassroots campaign, this young politician is unafraid to push back against the status quo. Regardless of how you feel about her policies, there's no denying that she refuses to play by the rules and young people are relating to her rebellion.

Youth support Ocasio-Cortez because she is one of them. She speaks her mind, does things her own way and is paving the path for political change. They will follow a leader like her. In general, however, young people are refusing to play previously established games in which the rules make no sense to them. They won't follow leaders who don't update the game board.

This movement began with the millennials, who desired a work-life balance based upon flexibility. Their professional focus was less of a boss/employee relationship where daily productivity was heavily monitored and micromanaged, and they leaned more toward a deliverable/outcome approach in the workplace, based upon trust and mutual respect. They threw out the idea of "going to the office," instead placing value on autonomy. *Where* and *how* you get the job done is up to you, as long as the job gets done on time. Rather than a strongly defined hierarchy of importance and power, millennials preferred the idea of people coming together and working as a team toward a shared goal. They wanted flexibility and connection, purpose and culture.

Essentially, they created tribes focused on similar beliefs, values, passions and principles. Millennials—and even more so those in Gen Z—are not looking for a leader. They are looking to each other, as equals.

Technology has made the creation of tribes and the connection of people an easy feat, and it's been surprisingly good for business. The talent pool has reached incredible depths, and with it, possibilities have opened up exponentially. Regardless of where employees are scattered across the globe, technology has made collaboration and conversation possible. It's no wonder young people turn up their noses at the idea of sitting at a desk trapped in a cubicle all day. Covid-19 has rendered the traditional work space extinct... and deservedly so!

Many of us, having had the opportunity to work remotely during the Covid-19 pandemic, can no longer dispute the benefits of working from home. Young people weren't lazy. They were wise. And, thanks to online platforms such as Zoom and Teams, we are able to experience the dual pleasures of productivity and comfort without the commute—a new and delightful work environment for many.

Covid-19 has shown us there is validity to what the millennials were craving. We all benefit from flexibility and team support. Just like how youth are examining political systems and socially prescribed norms, they are also looking at corporations. What they are seeing is an outdated structure, where the power is concentrated at the top. Living in a fast-paced, chaotic world, people, corporations and even countries need to be agile and forward thinking. We need to change the structure so we can make quick assessments and pivot when we need to. This is what inspired me to explore how the new world is forming leaderless organizations and teams.

When I began to research the concept of 'leaderless' teams, I came across an article that shared the following story,[28] which I will paraphrase for the sake of convenience.

> *In the 1500s, Spanish conquistadors sailed to Latin America only to be greeted by the peaceful Inca tribe. Upon arriving in this new land, the Spaniards demanded to meet with the leader of the Incas, who obliged his guests politely. The Spaniards promptly shot and killed the leader,*

---

28   "Starfish, Spiders, Cows, Geronimo the Apache and Entrepreneurial Start ups," (Conor Neill, October 18, 2009),https:// conorneill.com/2009/10/18/starfish-spiders-cows-geronimo-the-apache-and-entrepreneurial-start-ups/

declaring, "I am your new emperor." The Incas were soon wiped off the face of the planet, their culture, language and community utterly devastated.

A few short years later, Spanish conquistadors reached Baja, California and were greeted by the Apache tribe. Following the successful desecration of the Incas, the Spaniards used the same wartime strategy, attempting to arrange a meeting with the tribe's leader. There was only one problem— the Apaches had no leader.

The tradition of the Apache warriors allowed the freedom to follow whomever they deemed worthy. They followed whoever they wanted, whenever they wanted. When a "leader" died, the warriors split off into subgroups, following a new "leader." Two hundred years after meeting the Spaniards, the Apache tribe was still unconquered, still thriving.

This story seems to illustrate the cardinal difference between old and new ways of doing business. The antiquated way of thinking is where we follow an all-knowing, micromanaging leader figure. Subsequently—and problematically—if the leader falls, so does the organization. Perhaps there is some value to having flexibility when it comes to who we choose to follow. The story implies that the ability to adapt and pivot are essential to long term survival.

The story inspired me to investigate companies that seemed (from the outside), as close to "leaderless" as possible. The TED Talk organization seems to have erupted all over the world and takes the onus off an all-knowing, all-controlling guru and places it on the local organization. Any town or city can host a TED Talk—independently run within the approved parameters—and post content online, for free, under the mission statement that these are "ideas worth spreading."

It seems that the TED Foundation checks off some of the boxes in terms of following a leaderless philosophy—no one makes a profit and the power to organize is given to the people for the sake of knowledge and inspiration. Yet, TED organizers must follow strict rules as to the look and feel of each event, ensuring it holds true to the TED brand. Additionally, someone (currently Chris Anderson) is required to oversee the TED Foundation, continuing to uphold the creator's vision and intent. So, when there are rules, regulations and a CEO position, can we say that the organization is truly leaderless?

Next, I came across a website called Indivisible.org that provides a blueprint for grassroots organizations to take political action and "save democracy" from corrupt leadership. The website decrees that, "Local groups build and wield power in ways individuals can't. To create change, you need the power that comes with working together. We need to take action in our communities, build collective purpose and create change." Finally, I found what I'd been looking for—an organization that gave power to the people and was willing to teach them how to take ownership of the dilemma in ineffective government. However, a closer look reveals that they, too, have a board of directors.

My research then led me to a website called leaderless.co, which seems to embody the mentality of today's youth. When you first arrive at the site, you are greeted by a series of rhetorical questions:

> *What if we could rebuild trust using technology?*
> *What if we could decentralize society?*
> *What if we could build businesses with purpose?*

Their mission statement reveals a collective disappointment with ineffective and out-of-touch leaders that have failed society, and encourages individuals to take ownership of their lives and their communities by removing hierarchies and focusing, instead, on collaboration. They provide information on topics such as "decentralized innovation villages", "building mindful networks" and "teaching youth how to disrupt the adults."

Instead of a board of directors, they refer to their organizing team as "chiefs."

Villages, chiefs, youth and disruption? Now you're speaking my language! Perhaps they are on the right track. Still, chiefs are considered to be leaders in their communities.

After wracking my brain, the closest example of a leaderless organization I can come up with is, perhaps, the crypto currency known as Bitcoin. The person or group who is responsible for this innovation is unknown. The creator goes by the name of Satoshi Nakamoto, which many believe is a pseudonym. Furthermore, Bitcoin does not belong to a central bank and is not organized by a single administrator. Instead, "transactions are verified by network nodes through cryptography and recorded in a public distributed ledger called a blockchain."

No known founder, not part of the centralized banking world, no headquarters, no staff, no board of directors—Bitcoin seems to buck the system and functions independently without direct management, control or affiliation. It's all about a common mission with shared values and agreed upon guidelines. I see Bitcoin as a torch-bearer, leading us into the new world.

WHAT'S WORTH HOLDING ON TO?

As someone who prides himself on being a Young Elder, I am beginning to wonder if leaders are becoming an endangered species. Do we have enough time to change, adapt and maintain our relevance? How do we position ourselves in this new world? These are the hard questions I am grappling with, even as I write this book.

Isn't the existence of a person with vision and organizational skills necessary? Surely, someone needs to initiate the collaboration. Someone needs to sense a purpose and put the call out for a tribe to gather. Ideas don't spark out of thin air— they are the result of the conversations of innovators, or the brainchild of an individual.

> Leaders are becoming an endangered species.

Perhaps, instead of attempting to be truly leaderless, what is required is the redefining of the word "leader." As youth demand inclusivity, diversity, autonomy and individuality it creates a context where the traditional leadership role is rendered irrelevant. Perhaps the tradition is no longer worth holding onto. Just like schools are adopting a design thinking model and teachers are becoming facilitators instead of instructors, perhaps other forms of leadership need to follow this evolution. The all-knowing, micromanaging, dictatorial leader is being replaced by leaders who listen, delegate and guide their team toward success. The leader may be the creator of the vision who shares knowledge and experience in an effort to empower—rather than take power away.

Ironically, when I'm anxious about something new, I often find that the answers lie in the ancient world. In this instance, I look toward the biblical story of Abraham as the founder of transformational leadership. Abraham had no ego. He accepted everyone through the doors of his tent and worked to empower all those around him. He exemplified the concept of servant leadership.

I love the term servant leadership because it seems so paradoxical. How can one be both a leader and a servant?

This type of leader is a visionary, but is not afraid to get their hands dirty, leading by example. They do not govern from

above, perched upon a pedestal, but they are on the ground—
working alongside their people, hoping to achieve a common
goal. Their presence is strong, yet quiet. Certain, yet willing to
meet others where they are. They are influential, yet humble.
Think of Gandhi, Mother Teresa and Nelson Mandela. This
type of leadership seems sacred—a combination of experience,
wisdom, vision and trust.

WHAT DOES THIS MEAN?

> "As we look ahead into the next century,
> leaders will be those who empower others."
> BILL GATES

If we want to connect with youth, harness their brilliance and
set them up for success, we must be willing to be open to
leading in a different way. The question is, how do we take
the model of the humble, servant leader and transplant those
values into our modern day homes and businesses? One way
to start is to look around us for people who are already leading
by example—people who are trailblazing, subscribing to a
new way of thinking. These innovative leaders are showing
us the way.

Frederic Laloux

This author is well known for his progressive views on
restructuring businesses and flattening the hierarchy curve.

He is pioneering a new methodology. Laloux argues that small businesses and large corporations alike, are capable of restructuring in a way that increases employee autonomy and buy-in simply by focusing on self-management. He explains that, in expressing professional discontent, the youth are not meaning to be disrespectful to the establishment, but are simply longing for a workplace that moves away from micromanagement, pressure and stress, and moves toward freedom, balance and an environment where everyone is valued for what they bring to the table. The youth are voicing concerns that many executives have felt, but are too afraid to admit.

Morning Star

Morning Star is the world's largest tomato processing organization, a $700 million enterprise. They supply over 40% of the global market with tomato paste and diced tomatoes. Despite being an enormous conglomerate, at Morning Star, everyone is his or her own boss. Anyone can spend company money and employees negotiate salaries and responsibilities with each other. Why does this leaderless model succeed? Because "the mission is the boss."[29] As noted on their website, all employees are working toward the mission of, "producing tomato products which consistently achieve the quality and

---

29   "The Leaderless Organization," (Greg Satell, December 2, 2012), https://digitaltonto.com/2012/the-leaderless-organization/.

service expectations of our customers in a cost-effective, environmentally responsible manner."

Other Leaderless organizations to follow:[30]

- The Beverly Cooperative Bank (Massachusetts, USA)
- Lynetten Wind Cooperative (Denmark)
- Organic Valley (a group of more than 1,600 farmers in Wisconsin)

LEADING WITHOUT AUTHORITY

Effective leaders inspire through action. They share their beliefs and values through their thoughts, words and actions. Effective leaders share power and control, trusting in those around them. They consider the perspectives of others and keep an open mind toward new and unfamiliar ideas. Effective leaders are humble. They empower others

by encouraging them to follow their own passions. Effective leaders inspire by ushering

the group from behind, reminding them of the common goal, rather than forging ahead and pulling the others along forcefully. They influence through service.

---

30   "When No One's in Charge," (Andrea Ovans, May 2012), https://hbr.org/2012/05/when-no-ones-in-charge.

Instead of rejecting this new idea of leadership and clinging to old ways because they are familiar and safe, perhaps we could allow for some space to discover what may happen if we changed our ways. If we chose to lead quietly—to value the strengths and knowledge of our employees, to foster a community of trust, to be a chief instead of a commander— what possibilities would open up? Whether we lead in business, in politics, in humanitarianism, in family or in friendship— in order to be effective, we need to meet people where they are, and appeal to their values and beliefs instead of forcing them to conform in a way that doesn't ring true for them. We need to leave room for the possibility that our way may not be the best way, and nurture relationships that are reciprocal in nature. Yes, we have wisdom and experience to share, but could it be that we also have things to learn?

In his book *Leading Without Authority*, Keith Ferrazzi writes, "No single manager has the capacity to meet the demands of this fast-paced, competitive world,"[3] and it's true. This is why flattening the hierarchical structure of power and influence in favor of collaborative teams is crucial in today's workplace. Ferrazzi declares that a leader's ability to transform their teams will inevitably "transform the world." The implementation of collaborative teams has produced numerous benefits, Ferrazzi explains—including better sales, higher employee productivity, increased levels of innovation, deeper employee engagement, as well as increased revenue and profitability.

The reason for their success is twofold, according to Ferrazzi. Firstly, considering the fast pace of the business world, a team approach allows companies to respond quickly to changing needs. Teams have the ability to "cut through bureaucratic bottlenecks of authority to achieve better, faster results."[3] Essentially, if the hierarchy is flattened, employee expertise is trusted, and the power of decision-making is shared, companies are able to adapt and make change as needed, instead of lagging behind while waiting for approvals. Secondly, taking a team approach to business immediately widens the scope of innovation and problem solving by increasing "insights exponentially instead of just those of a few higher ups."[3] Allowing for more opinions, different perspectives and encouraging deeper employee engagement creates space for new ideas that may not have come up if the brainstorming was relegated to a select few. The best leaders ask good questions then "start with an open mind and invite others to seek solutions with them."[31]

So, perhaps it's not necessary that all organizations go entirely leaderless, but instead embrace a collaborative team structure. Even if we don't go leaderless, we can certainly go leader-LESS. Leaders need to be strong now—in a different way; they need to release control and make it okay to be human in the workplace, while driving their teams with inspired thinking toward greatness.

---

31   "Leading Without Authority: How the New Power of Co-Elevation Can Break Down Silos, Transform Teams, and Reinvent Collaboration," (Keith Ferrazzi and Noel Weyrich, May 26, 2020)

Perhaps the idea of a leaderless society is not so much advocating the absence of a leader as it is the reshaping of the front-runner—with LESS ego. LESS bravado. LESS control. MORE transparency. MORE empathy. MORE creative collaboration.

TIPS AND TAKEAWAYS

- Consider how your company can flatten the hierarchal curve, empowering employees and providing autonomy and flexibility

- Take a look at technologies that will support this new leadership style

- Ask yourself how you can practice servant leadership—use influence instead of power and be humble

- Create teams that empower those who work with you

- Leaders need to be more present, but show up in a different way that is more authentic and more vulnerable

CHAPTER TWELVE
THE FUTURE OF MANAGEMENT: "MOM-AGERS"

Mom-agers. This might be the next position you post in your human resources department.

What is a mom-ager? It's exactly what it sounds like—a manager who interacts with colleagues with all the patience and compassion of a mother.

One of the complaints I hear frequently from companies is that young people make terrible employees. They are needy, require way too much support and reassurance, and want instant gratification. After all, when youth ask Siri a question, she answers immediately. Why can't their managers do the same?

With young people in the workplace, their demands can feel like a frustrating game of opposites—help me, but don't micromanage. Be interested in me, but don't smother. Guide me toward greatness but don't boss me around. Many employers are finding it exhausting and difficult to manage.

Why do youth come to the workplace with such a strong need for validation, acknowledgment and nurturing? I believe the answer lies in two areas of their upbringing—the drastic change of family dynamics, and the way in which their parents were overprotective of them as children.

There's no denying that the nature of families has changed, with many of today's youth being raised in non-traditional households. In recent generations, the concept of a traditional nuclear family has been eroded. In many parts of the world almost half of marriages don't work out. Thus, youth are being raised by a multitude of people who have created family units that are not bound by previous societal expectations. Gen Z may be raised by single parents, same sex parents, grandparents or foster parents.[32] Depending on what part of the world you are from, many households are absent of a father-figure and

---

32   "Children in single-parent families by race in the United States," (The Annie E. Casey Foundation, 2021), https://tinyurl.com/b7u4mzmd.

children are being raised solely by women.[33] In other parts of the world where fathers may be present, they are more involved than ever before, taking on a traditionally feminine role. Dads are becoming more like moms—sharing household and parenting duties.

Whether young people were raised in households with doting parents or absent ones, they are walking into the workplace looking for the parental relationship they idolized as children. If they didn't receive nurturing and support in their homes, they believe their managers will be the ones to fill this void. If they were raised by helicopter parents, they are primed to expect this same treatment at work. Protectively wrapping children in cotton wool has created young people who demand "cotton wool careers."

Now, consider the fact that most of us who are current world leaders, corporate executives and business owners were brought up in traditional households and subjected to very narrow gender expectations. Many of our current leaders are men, or women who have adopted a male energy in order to climb the ladder of success and power. The traditional father role has become symbolic of our current leadership—a heavy hand with high expectations—complete with disregard for mental health and an emphasis on profit over people (outcome based, be tough, work harder). With many of our youth entering the

---

33   "How Many Women Worldwide Are Single Moms?," (Steve Crabtree and Sofia Kluch, March 5, 2020), https://news.gallup.com/poll/286433/women-worldwide-single-moms.aspx.

workplace only knowing a nurturing, compassionate motherly energy, a chasm of disconnect between the generations is inevitable.

Older generations pride ourselves on having worked hard to earn our status. We often did it alone, without coddling. Young people want constant guidance and reassurance (traits our parenting has created). This is the source of the disconnect.

Many current leaders complain that youth are lazy, disengaged, and averse to authority. I'd like to suggest that this is not entirely true. Unaccustomed to a fatherly energy, young people are simply searching for a different kind of manager.

They desire a **MOM-AGER.**

As previously suggested, youth are resistant to having a commander, but not to having a chief. They desire autonomy but wish to feel safe and supported. They want to be trusted, so wish for their managers to remain at a distance, available when needed—like their mothers were. They need someone to provide perspective, to show them the way. They need patience, understanding and caring. Young people will follow a strong leader, but the strength they desire is shown in a different way. Youth crave a chief with strong values and a strong vision. They appreciate someone who cultivates strong relationships. What Generation Z is averse to, is a chief who gets strong *on them.*

> Young people are simply searching for a
> different kind of manager.

When it comes to workplace discipline, managers cannot come down on their colleagues with the same harsh honesty that we received when we were young employees. For many young people, failure is their worst fear—something they have been protected against their whole lives—and hard discipline inevitably hits their shame button. The possibility of failure, coupled with the disappointment of an elder, opens deep wounds—inducing a mourning period and the road to recovery can be a long one. When we come in hard with discipline, we breach their trust.

Generation Z is conflict averse and they view our willingness to engage in difficult conversations as aggressive. Young people prefer to text or email their issues instead of having a face-to-face conversation. Ideally, they'd love to outsource it to someone else. Courageous conversations are unbearable—a last resort for them—something their parents would have handled for them when they were children. So, when it comes to disciplining our employees and having uncomfortable conversations with them, taking a mom-ager approach will be more effective and avoids shame, withdrawal, guilt and hopefully moves toward progress.

A mom-ager approaches discipline with compassion and patience. They take the time to hear various perspectives in an effort to understand the *why and how* behind any given situation. They help employees see the big picture, and guide them to see the impact of their choices and actions. Feedback is constructive and intended to nurture colleagues toward improvement.

Some readers may argue that the fast pace of business is not always conducive to such time-consuming mentoring and others may scold young people for being needy. I don't disagree with you and in fact, I caution you not to underestimate the energy this type of leadership takes. It's an additional, invisible load in the workplace. While I validate your concerns, I also want to caution you—like it or not, these are the needs young people are bringing into the workplace. While we can ask ourselves how much bandwidth we have to offer when it comes to emotional support, we cannot disregard the needs of an entire generation. If youth are not receiving what they feel they require to grow and thrive, they will simply leave and we will miss out on their talent.

The question becomes, how much support is enough?

WHAT DOES THIS MEAN?

It may be easier to begin with what this does *not* mean. My suggestion that youth desire a mom-ager does not mean you are required to hold their hands and walk on eggshells. It does not mean that you are forbidden to disagree, correct, provide feedback or discipline. Let's be honest—workplaces involve expectations, independence, deadlines, dedication and a high level of performance. If an employee is not towing the line and is letting others down, that needs to be addressed. It does not mean that you can't uphold your standards and the needs of your organization. What matters is *how* you do it.

What I am suggesting is that hard conversations are easier to have when you have already worked to establish a healthy relationship with your colleagues. If you are the type of manager who sits in your office, away from your coworkers, and only emerges to aggressively point out missteps and use shame tactics as your primary source of motivation, chances are, your employees are not working hard to please you. They are working to avoid you.

Alternatively, if you create a workplace culture based on empathy, connection, and belonging, when a situation arises that requires you to point out underperformance, the employee may be willing to listen because you are working on a foundation of trust and respect. Mom-agers interact with honesty and compassion. They celebrate success and support during failure, always reminding them about the bigger picture. They encourage reflection and offer perspective. Youth are not against correction, they simply want to feel accepted and supported.

Think about a mother and her small child visiting a playground. The mother steps back and allows the child to explore, smiling, waving and encouraging when the child looks her way. If the child climbs too high, the mother will step forward and help the child develop a plan that is safe and will allow them to feel successful. Then she steps back and encourages the child to keep climbing. If the child throws sand at a playmate, the mother steps forward to gently remind the child of expected behavior. She does not shame or embarrass, but asks the child to remember expectations and go forth making better choices. Then she steps back again. The mother is always within reach but does not hover or control. Simply knowing she is there to help, when needed, is what gives the child confidence.

In the first years of parenting, your child is never out of your sight. You are right beside them, coaching, supporting, teaching and protecting. When you are raising teenagers, you may not be physically with them, but you are available at all times—phone always on, ready to spring into action when necessary. In the workplace, a mom-ager operates in much the same way—being present and encouraging as employees are learning, then taking small steps back and forth when support is needed. They may not be physically present but are always available.

Perhaps what young people desire isn't entirely unreasonable at the core. They just need it in excess. In the corporate world, how many of us lamented that we were underappreciated and undervalued? How many of us felt frustrated by the lack of validation in the workplace? No one likes to feel unseen or unheard. Yes, youth may lack tact when advocating for their needs. Yes, their needs require a change in attitude from those of us higher on the corporate ladder, but I ask you, are those changes necessarily a bad thing? Wouldn't we all like to work in an environment where we feel connectedness, belonging, trust and validation? Wouldn't we all like to be coached and guided and then be given the space to explore and master our skills?

Generation Z might be right in their needs. The problem is how much of this need is acceptable? While companies should acknowledge this desire and take it on, increasing their bandwidth for employee support, the bandwidth is not unlimited. Mom-agers should set boundaries for availability and be clear about expectations. They can help young people differentiate between personal and professional roles. Yes, we are a family at work, but this family does not offer unconditional love. There are conditions and standards to uphold in this relationship. Within these boundaries, supportive mom-agers are essentially "raising" our future leaders.

Now that you have a greater understanding of your young employees, I urge you to take a moment to reflect on your own mom-ager qualities. Consider the following:

Are you available?

Are you compassionate?

Do you provide encouragement?

Do you provide autonomy?

Do you build relationships with your employees?

Is your feedback meant to criticise or inspire growth?

Is your discipline meant to shame or teach?

Are you a mom-ager, a dictator, aloof, or something in between?

TIPS AND TAKEAWAYS

- Make yourself available but have healthy boundaries in place

- Offer lots of support but don't micromanage.

- Find ways to foster healthy relationships with your colleagues—make time to get to know them on a personal level but don't get sucked into their personal dramas

- Provide honest feedback but not too honest—it may induce a mourning period

- Use compassionate discipline but don't forget to land the consequences of their underperformance

- Understand that being a mom-ager can be overwhelming but don't forget that you are allowed to be transparent about what you are feeling and can defer while you regain your composure

- The more vulnerable you are, the more they will understand you and the more real your relationship with them will be

PART 2

THE ROLE OF
THE ELDERS

CHAPTER THIRTEEN
WHAT IS YOUR LEADERSHIP STYLE?

Epic battles often begin with two opposing sides fighting for power and control. Negotiations may start in a friendly manner, but tend to take an ugly turn when goals are opposing. Imagine, for example, aliens arriving on Earth for the first time. They land their spaceship and upon exiting, encounter a human being. The aliens look at this interesting species and call out, "Take me to your leader." The aliens want to take over the planet, causing the humans to rise up in defense.

Earlier in the book, I shared a story of Spanish conquerors, who used this same simple tactic to overthrow and decimate entire populations of natives. "Take me to your leader." they said. The natives did not go down quietly.

Imagine youth, walking up to the establishment and demanding a conversation. "Take me to your leader," they say. "If I were in charge…" they begin.

When we were young, many elders had the exact same thoughts—just how different things would be if they were in control. Young people often feel misunderstood. They hold a strong belief that the leaders do not represent their needs, wants, values or vision. They call for change and insist that if the elders do not adapt, youth will remove the leadership and replace it with one of their own. "We can do this the easy way or the hard way," they say.

We caught a glimpse of this sentiment during the initial phases of Covid-19. Companies that survived and began to thrive were those who were quick to respond to the crisis, or who were already entrenched in a flexible and autonomous way of working. Companies who struggled held on to an outdated business structure, or were already destined for a decline that was simply accelerated by the pandemic. Some companies wish they had seen the signs and taken action earlier and many made a reluctant pivot because the only other option was professional death.

In retrospect, we can give kudos to the millennials, who had flexibility and autonomy as their rally cry for years before Covid. They saw the future of the workplace. They were right. We also need to acknowledge the elders who listened, accommodated and adapted. Their willingness to change their ways saved their companies.

Traditional leadership roles depict elders who are the knowers of all things, the holders of wisdom of which they will pass down to younger generations. In business, we may call it mentorship—an arrangement where the elder provides advice and shows youth how things are properly done. I'd like to suggest this is old world thinking. If we learned anything from Covid, it's that mentorship can and should be reciprocal. It's an elder who explains successful business practices and a young person who responds, "Did you know there's an app for that?" In being open to hearing a new way of doing things, the elder may realize that the app could save both time and money. When we realize that both sides have expertise to offer and that knowledge is not just a one-way street, companies thrive and epic battles can be avoided.

> Mentorship can and should be reciprocal

TAKING A LOOK IN THE LEADERSHIP MIRROR

Before we dive into the future of leadership or—by contrast—leaderlessness, I believe it's important to understand what type of leader you already are, what your preconceptions about leadership may be and your current leadership style. I encourage you to take a judgement-free approach to this

section of the book. Be honest with yourself about what beliefs you currently hold and what habits you have developed over time. It's important for us to be aware of our blind spots in order to evolve and choose how we want to lead in the future.

Braden Becker describes the following types of leadership in an article titled, "The 8 Most Common Leadership Styles and How to Find Your Own."[34]

> **Democratic leadership:** The leader makes decisions based on the input and opinions of others. While the leader considers the perspectives of team members, he/she retains the right to make the final call.
>
> **Autocratic leadership:** Similar to an authoritarian style of leadership, where the leader takes the role of a dictator and does not consider the input or opinions of others.
>
> **Laissez faire leadership:** Literally translates to "let them do." These leaders delegate power and authority to their team members, trusting their autonomy.
>
> **Strategic leadership:** Where the leader accepts the burden of executive interests while ensuring

---

34   "The 8 Most Common Leadership Styles & How to Find Your Own," (Braden Becker, February 7, 2020), https://blog.hubspot.com/marketing/leadership-styles.

that current working conditions remain stable for everyone else.

Transformational leadership: Values growth and encourages team members to push through their comfort zones to achieve something new.

Transactional leadership: involves a reward system, recognizing employees for a job well done.

Coach style leadership: identifies individual strengths of team members and creates strategies based on skills and passion areas.

Bureaucratic leadership: Probably the most traditional style of leadership, where input is listened to, but rejected if it threatens company policy or the way things have been done in the past.

Perhaps you may see yourself in one or more of these leadership styles. Now, I'd like to challenge you to participate in a less traditional exercise—one that's equally valuable, but takes a more creative approach to introspection.

Author Lara Hogan chooses to differentiate leadership styles through the use of colors and encourages reflection through a list of guiding questions.[35]

---

35   "Leadership Style Colors," (Lara Hogan, July 9, 2018), https://larahogan.me/blog/leadership-style-colors/

Red	A bit of anger, frustration, edge, or urgency
Orange	Cautious, hesitant, tiptoes, low-risk
Yellow	Lighthearted, effervescent, cracks jokes
Green	In tune with feelings, loving, high EQ
Blue	Calm, cool, collected, steady
Purple	Creative, flowy, great at storytelling
Brown	Adds (and lives in) nuance, complexity, or ambiguity
Black	Blunt, unfeeling, no nuance, cut and dry

- What's your default leadership style? (What color would you call it?)
- What other leadership styles are you comfortable leaning on?
- What leadership style is the hardest for you to embody or project?
- Which of these drain you?
- Which energizes you?
- Which do you know you should use more of, but rarely do?
- How does your leadership style appear to others?
- What's the effect that it has on those around you?
- What energy does it create in your environment?

- What is it that you're embodying?

Just as childhood shaped who we are as people, our career journey is formed by our own beliefs and by those who lead us. Leadership styles are forged by our past experiences. In our youth, our experience at any particular company was directly linked to our relationships with our managers. We took note of leadership traits that motivated us and traits which degraded, frustrated and angered us. "That leader inspires me," is equally formative as, "I will never behave that way." We are products of what we felt, experienced and observed.

So, where do we go from here?

I'm not about to ask you to throw away everything that has been working well for you. I am simply asking you to expand your understanding of leadership and to entertain the concept of leaderlessness. I am about to suggest that, in order to remain a relevant, respected and influential leader, you may need to redefine your role while simultaneously embracing your strengths.

LEADING WITH A HUMAN TOUCH

We've discussed the idea of masculine versus feminine leadership and you read about the notion of a gentler, more compassionate leadership style—which resonates well with our youth.

Braden Becker defines "coach-style leadership", as a style that helps people shine in their zone of genius in a way that benefits a team. This leadership style focuses on authenticity, personal awareness and trust. The way a mom-ager would be attuned to, and understand, their team and how to harness their greatness, is akin to the way a mom would understand her own kids.

Lara Hogan identifies a few feminine leadership traits such as creativity, flowy and storytelling. This type of leadership allows for some ebb and flow, or give and take. Guidelines are not rigid, nor restricting, but encourage team members to explore and take risks in a safe, supportive environment that allows failure—just as a mom would nurture her kids.

In her book, *We Can: The Executive Woman's Guide to Career Advancement,* author Robin Toft, takes a deep dive into the concept of leading with femininity.[36] While she writes for a largely-female audience, I believe her ideas align with a gender-fluid generation, seeking a specific style of leader.

According to Toft, feminine leadership embodies the following qualities:

- Valuing debate and weighing options before making a decision
- Encouraging self-care for both leaders and team members

---

36   "We Can: The Executive Woman's Guide to Career Advancement," (Robin Toft, February 2019), https://www. merackpublishing.com/we-can

- Knowing your team, so that you may motivate them effectively and understand how they can make the greatest contributions to the whole
- Solutions-based problem solving
- Vulnerability and transparency
- Fostering teamwork and collaboration
- Authenticity

In contrast, leading with a masculine energy is less about collaboration and care, and more about stubborn assuredness and a sense of drive. Masculine leadership is focused, driven and goal oriented. There is a clear vision, a predefined path to achievement, and an inspirational passion that fires everyone up. Many people find that this type of leadership feels secure. There is a definite chain of command and a confident elder who holds all the answers. Others may find it stifling—robbing them of creativity.

In tandem with your exploration of leadership styles outlined by Becker and Hogan, it may be a useful exercise to consider whether or not you lean toward a masculine or feminine energy in your leadership philosophy and interactions with your team. While most teams thrive when guided by leaders who straddle both sets of traits, in times of stress and anxiety, we tend to regress into our default coping styles—feminine leaders relying too heavily on the opinions of others and masculine leaders grasping for control.

Now that you are more aware of your own strengths and challenges in your leadership style, let's see how it stacks up with what young people desire. In the next few chapters, we will explore what youth really want from their elders.

TIPS AND TAKEAWAYS

- Start by taking an honest, non-judgmental look at your leadership style

- Ask yourself if your leadership style fits the needs of the future direction of your organization

- Leaders need to have a combination masculine and feminine qualities

CHAPTER FOURTEEN

GUIDE ME TO MY GREATNESS: ELDERS AS FACILITATORS

A NEW DAY, A NEW DAWN

I believe it was Einstein who said (and I paraphrase), "A fish would spend its whole life thinking it were stupid, if it were judged on its ability to climb a tree."

We read that statement and exclaim, "Of course! How obvious!" Yet when I suggest that the future of this world requires a different kind of leadership, people falter. They fall back upon what they know and they cling to what has worked in the past. If you take anything away from this book, I hope it is this: Young people think differently. They see the world differently. Thus, our relationship with them needs to be different.

In the course of this book, we have discussed various leadership styles. We learned that youth prefer nurturing "mom-agers", and that they look for a chief, but not a commander. I have used the term elder and suggested that our duty is to guide young people. We have even mulled over the concept of a leaderless society and questioned what that may look like. I'd like to begin this chapter by clarifying that, yes, I do believe leaders are necessary. I also believe the nature of future leadership is vastly different than it was in the past.

While the younger generations pride themselves on their ability to self-organize, to self-actualize and self-direct, they still require a person (or team of people) who can articulate the end goal. Today's leaders are visionaries and custodians of values. They are architects and facilitators, helping others understand where they matter and how they contribute to the collective goal. Then, leaders offer the freedom for their team to execute the vision in their own way—provided that it benefits the team as a whole. We inspire, then we step back. It's a gorgeous, delicate dance.

Elon Musk, one of the most profound innovators and entrepreneurs of our time is a prime example of someone who has perfected this dance. This industry disruptor encourages his teams to take risks, fail, and be creative while supporting and guiding them toward a shared goal. Take a moment to read his thoughts on leadership and consider how untraditional his views are. While he undoubtedly guides the big picture, he trusts his people and relies on their genius.

"People work better when they know what the goal is and why."

"Failure is an option here. If things are not failing, you are not innovating enough."

"A company is a group organized to create a product or service, and is only as good as its people and how excited they are about creating."

Elon Musk has shown us that by letting go of control, we allow our teams to thrive. In this way, leadership is often a position held not by one, but by many. It's no longer a position held by the people at the top. As the hierarchy flattens and more people have autonomy to make decisions, change happens quickly and younger leaders are more engaged. Committees can be formed to provide multiple people the opportunity to exercise a leadership role based on their personal genius and areas of expertise. When leadership ebbs and flows—varying by passion and skill—the results are often astounding.

Regardless of a single visionary or a shared vision, all effective leaders should strive to let go of control and allow others to take the lead. This, I know, is counterintuitive—it's called lead-ership, after all. I believe that the best leaders do not lead at all. They follow. They are virtually invisible. Hear me out...

GUIDE ME TO MY GREATNESS

We have already established that youth prefer a leader who is emotionally intelligent, who removes judgement and serves to empower others. A leader sets the tone, paints the picture and articulates the values. A leader is inclusive, communicative and collaborative. This is a great start but I'd like to suggest something different.

> What if a leader is not a leader at all?

As elders learn to let go of control and to instill trust in their teams, they shed the role of traditional leadership and begin to emerge as facilitators.

One definition of the word "facilitator" reads as follows, "A person who helps a group of people to work together better, to understand common objectives and plan how to achieve these objectives… In doing so, the facilitator remains neutral, meaning he or she does not take a particular position in the discussion." I also came across this definition, which hits the message home, "A facilitator is the one who makes things easier." Omit "facilitator" and insert "guide" into both of these definitions and there you have it—a modern leader for today's youth.

Notice the first definition requires guides to abstain from holding their own position or personal agenda. The absence of intrusiveness is integral to effective guidance. If we lead with a plan in mind, we become old-school leaders who dictate or manipulate in order to bring the vision into fruition. We are holding judgment and fighting for control. We are not trusting our team. We are essentially making the process more difficult, which violates the guide's foundational role of fostering ease and a safe space. When we diffuse judgment and allow for the truth to emerge, we can make meaningful decisions. The conversation needs to flow organically and free from fear in order to be effective and innovative. For this reason, guides never provide the answer. As soon as leaders share the answer, conversation grinds to a halt. The what ifs, the imagining and the wondering stop. Instead of sharing the answer, we provide perspective, wisdom and provocative questions that unlock the realm of collaboration, communication and creativity.

And so, the guide—the "one who makes things easier"— empowers young people by orchestrating a safe discussion space and by elevating the group as a whole. The guide holds an inherent understanding that this process is not about him/her, but is about the good of the group. As perspectives are shared and solutions begin to emerge, the guide withholds his/her own opinions and gives the power back to the group, allowing them to make decisions collectively. In this way, the group essentially becomes leaderless.

This isn't revolutionary thinking. It's simply a healthy next step, or maybe a current step for some. Leaderless companies have diluted top-down power and have shared the responsibility and trust so that leaders can emerge *throughout* the organization. While this way of thinking may seem logical and appealing—it looks great on paper!—making this transition in your company won't come without its growing pains. It will be hard, but it is possible and it is important.

In the next **section** of this book, I will share my own journey toward becoming leaderless and will divulge all of the hesitations, fears, doubts and triumphs I experienced in the process.

TIPS AND TAKEAWAYS

- It's not easy for a leader to step into the role of facilitation, it takes practice

- Diversity of opinions is crucial for innovation

- A mixture of young and tenured leadership is important

- Leave your own opinions out of the room, so as to not influence organic discussion of possibilities

- Ask thought-provoking questions, play Devil's Advocate and provide perspective

- Don't give away the answer, lead others to discover it for themselves

- Leaderlessness embodies the principle of less is more

SECTION 5:

A CASE STUDY

CHAPTER FIFTEEN
BEFORE THE CHANGE

WALKING THE WALK

One of my primary goals was to make this book practical. I tend to be a big thinker, dreaming about how I might impact the world around me and how I might inspire others to do the same. I realize that some of you might think there is nothing new here, or that this will be too hard to achieve. I hear you. When I realized what I needed to do, I felt sick to my stomach as a wave of nausea came over me. It was a realization that the very thing that irritated me about how my family business was run was what I had become—a modified version of *that*. I hadn't evolved as much as I thought.

We need to understand that the next generation is already flowing into the workplace and challenging the leadership styles of the Elders. This dynamic is not going to get any easier unless we are willing to take a hard look in the mirror. It's not just about the young people who are coming in, it's also about the changing world and its rapid pace. Many of us have been looking at youth as the crux of the problem—but the opposite is true. They are part of the solution and we need to change in order to harness their power.

> I hadn't evolved as much as I thought.

As I was writing this book, I searched for a case study to illustrate that leaderlessness—though complicated—can be done. I could have looked at the biggest companies to see how they are restructuring their teams. But I realized that there's no way I could write this book with any authenticity unless I took a long, hard look at myself. It's definitely easier to look externally but the path I wanted to focus on was an internal journey of change. For a leader like myself, this type of transformation questions every single belief you ever held about yourself and your organization. It will keep you up at night. It will cause you to face your own mortality as a leader. Despite the fact that this was going to be a terrifying and excruciating process, I believe that changing one's default settings is difficult, but not impossible, and it will be so rewarding if you succeed.

For the last twenty years, I had been an old-school leader. I made all of the decisions. At Student Village, I was acting as the CFO, the COO, the CEO, the C-Everything and it was exhausting. I was burnt out. I was doing so many things at once, it was preventing me from doing what I actually love. It had been a very long time since I had the time or the energy to operate in my zone of genius—to create and inspire. This left me not only tired, but resentful.

And so, it is with great humility—and a little embarrassment—that I choose to offer myself as the case study for this book. I had talked the talk for a long time now, and it was about time that I began to walk the walk.

Case study: Ronen Aires and Student Village

THE EMERGING FACILITATOR

Here's the truth about me. I love concepts and ideating, but I do not like the day-to-day grind of running the business. Twenty years ago, when we started Student Village, I was blessed with two business partners. We were able to play off of each other's strengths and compensate for areas of weakness. We were able to dream of a platform that would reach out to, inspire and support youth who were becoming independent for the first time in their lives. We dreamed of connecting youth with brands and mentors in the business world—people who would help the next generation of leadership rise up and meet their full potential. The goal was to create a meeting place for like-minded young people to connect with each other and with opportunity. We wanted to give youth a voice.

The partnership between the three of us worked well. My partners took care of all the details I hated—payroll, minute decision-making, human resources, systems and processes—things that would have stolen me away from my passions. They built the website and I nurtured client relationships and became the face of the company. The three of us were a well-oiled machine. But, over time, things changed and twenty years into this little project, I find myself the last man standing. My first partner exited in 2006 and the second one chose to move on at the end of 2019. A few months after his departure, Covid-19 struck and I soon found myself wondering if Student Village would survive all of this change.

Looking back, I can see that Covid-19 was a blessing because it accelerated the need for my company to innovate and to change the way we ran things. But at the moment, I couldn't see this. All I knew was that it felt like I was stuck under a massive rock. I was stuck in a scenario where I knew I needed to change but was in a mind space that was so depleted from simply trying to hold it all together that I couldn't see the answer.

I was so tired. I could no longer find the magic within myself— much less bring it out in others. Between an overwhelmingly full inbox and constantly being inundated with requests from employees asking for my approval on just about everything, I found myself thinking, "I don't fucking care." I had dedicated my whole adult life to the creation of Student Village and I found myself wondering if I had the will, or the energy, to change. I needed to adjust my leadership style. I had to shift the environment within the company. Pretty much everything needed a makeover. Student Village no longer represented my passion for being a Village Elder. It had become the bane of my existence. I had become a prisoner of my own creation.

As things got worse, I knew I needed to look at other options. I can generally endure painful situations for a long time and giving up was never an option. Even though I was completely depleted, I knew I had to push forward and that the journey would be excruciatingly tough.

The thing is, I aspire to be an effective facilitator. I'm a natural guide in the right environment. When things are going well at Student Village, I feel confident stepping back and letting my colleagues make choices, innovate and be creative. It's easy to facilitate in those moments. However, when in defense mode, my old wiring kicks in and then fear and control dominate. When I am not in a good headspace, I fall back onto dictatorship. It's like a switch—facilitator gone, commander and chief here to stay. My inner voice starts yelling, "No one else can do it like I can. I have the skill. I have the experience. I have the vision. No one will ever execute up to my standards." Then I take the reins and gain total control of the situation. I lose trust. I lose perspective. My inbox and my brain become overwhelmed and cluttered. Everything is a mess.

I become more controlling and so my team becomes increasingly disempowered. I'm not sure what came first, but it has created a nasty circle—and I am at the center of it.

Something needed to change. I needed to shake up the status quo so that I was no longer the commander but the facilitating Elder. My team and I needed to reorganize our corporate structure so that it was not just me at the top. Logically, I knew this. I even knew how to do it. So, why hadn't I done it? Because I was scared. This is precisely what makes my story an excellent case study.

EXCUSES

I had a hundred excuses for why this would not work—why I could not possibly become a facilitator at Student Village. I also knew that these represented a hundred fears I needed to push through in order to prove that my theory about youth and leaderlessness would actually work. It was time to put my money where my mouth was.

This **section** of the case study is meant to illustrate my frame of mind *before* creating change at Student Village. I acknowledge that this **section** will be a humbling and unflattering version of myself—certainly not the version that I want to be, or to portray to my readers. Despite this, it's who I was at that moment. I want to expose my fears in order to normalize them. Some of these fears had slivers of truth and some of it was just the narrative in my head. Either way, the last thing I want to do is leave you with the impression that adjusting your role from leader to facilitator is easy. It's not easy! I found it terrifying. Yet, I honestly believe the mess and uncertainty will be worth it. I'm going to prove it to myself and to you.

Excuse #1: In order for me to facilitate, my team needed to up their game.

Don't get me wrong, my team is excellent. They will most likely be offended by reading this, but I take full responsibility for our situation. I had micromanaged for so long, that my team had become superb doers but uninspired thinkers. The result of years of micromanaging had disempowered them. I needed to make all the decisions. They were not overly inspired, nor innovative—which is the result of not having the space or encouragement to do so. I had built a hierarchy where I was alone at the top. If I were to suddenly expect them to innovate or assume leadership, I would be setting them up for failure.

Letting go of control would involve a massive retraining of my team. They would need to be involved in every aspect of the rebuild and frankly, some of them are not cut out for the task. Some people may not buy into the new vision and might leave the team, others might be asked to leave if they didn't up their game. So, not only would we be restructuring processes and policies, but we would be forced to seek out fresh talent. Every time I considered the possibility of leaderlessness, the vision seemed to become more daunting.

Excuse #2: I couldn't change because things would fall apart.

In one of many painful conversations about my exhaustion with colleagues and friends, one dear friend dared me to simply quit being a boss and start being a facilitator by saying, "Just stop. Stop making decisions. Stop leading. Stop fixing things."

My gut response was shock and rage, "You can't be serious! Without me, everything will fall apart."

"Then let everything fall apart and you will see how your team builds it back up again."

Though the daredevil in me was tempted to do just that, there was too much at stake. I could not simply stop leading my team. First of all, I needed to uphold a level of excellence, which I was not willing to let go of simply because I was tired. If we let our standards slip, we would lose clients and if that happened, we would lose everything. There's no way I can expect my team to value Student Village to the extent that I do. This is my passion and my creation, but for them, it's a paycheck.

Secondly, the process of restructuring would take an incredible amount of time. It would have to happen little by little, not in one fell swoop. To simply stop being a leader would be disastrous. This was a mental block for me. I couldn't imagine letting Student Village break so that we could rebuild. I wasn't even tempted to try.

Excuse #3: It's one thing to reimagine and daydream, but the execution of that dream is an entirely different beast.

The big thinker in me absolutely loved the idea of involving my team in recreating a better, stronger, more collaborative Student Village. Hypothetically, it sounded great! What an empowering team building experience! Despite this, the gap between taking what I imagined, and making it our reality felt huge. I had a business to run. How could I possibly throw out the established way of doing things and restructure my entire business? I was just trying to make it through each day without losing my business—or my sanity.

I knew that in order to become leaderless, I would need to trust in the care my team had for Student Village and our past successes. I would need to tear down existing structures and implement systems and technologies that would allow people to operate in their genius without it becoming chaotic. I would probably need to say goodbye to some teammates. The thought of flipping everything on its head was debilitating but it was becoming ever more clear that it was the only choice I had.

MOVING FORWARD

I was cognizant of these fears—they kept me up at night—but despite all of it, I knew that if I didn't change the way things were done, it would mean the death of my company, my creativity, my passion and everything I ever valued. I was ready to push through the fear because I knew all the pain and discomfort would be worth it on the other side.

This decision felt like a rebirthing process—for myself as a leader, and for the business. It was a willingness to let go of everything that didn't serve us and the reimagining of who we could be as individuals, as a team and as a company.

I was preparing to step into my own greatness. It was time.

CHAPTER SIXTEEN
THE PLAN

I truly believed that once my team understood what I was offering—a leaderless union of peers—they would want to explore that opportunity. However, one of the challenges I anticipated is that not everyone would come to this realization at the same time. Most likely, there would be a lag between those who adopted the idea immediately and those who would need to slowly warm up to it.

I also understood that part of implementing this plan would mean that we might have to lose some of the team. At Student Village, we have always considered ourselves a family—a very unstructured, and sometimes dysfunctional, family. All members may not buy into this new version of our business and I anticipated some casualties of change.

Another huge area of concern was accountability. How could I relinquish control and set up an environment where the team kept each other accountable? I had seen this work in other companies, so I knew it was possible. Also, knowing how far down the road we were in our current hierarchy, this current system felt entrenched in our DNA. There was an element of doubt about whether we could make a drastic shift with the existing team. It felt easier to erase the current reality entirely and then start again, but that wasn't an option. I needed to figure out a way to create both flexibility and structure.

After much thought, my intuition told me three things.

1. Keeping each other accountable just wouldn't work. There's too much room for human emotion to derail us. We needed to devise a system of accountability that would eliminate human error. If expectations were clear, and roles and deliverables were defined, then we could execute with flair.

2. In order for my team to truly buy into our new culture and structure, they needed to co-create it.

3. To keep young people engaged and motivated, the work must be meaningful, growth-oriented and fun.

BREAKING FREE FROM THE COMMANDER AND CHIEF

I've mentioned that one of the strongest values at Student Village is family. This culture is strong, and people love it, but it has also been our biggest downfall. When you expect colleagues to keep each other accountable, familial emotions get in the way. Unconditional love brings a lack of accountability because no one wants to hurt someone else's feelings. We needed to upgrade our definition of family. We needed to be able to have hard conversations and maintain accountability—something Gen Z finds incredibly difficult.

As the father figure in this family, I was part of the problem. I am a creator at heart, a spontaneous guy—and I often bounce around, following ideas and passion. My lack of focus was reflected in my company. My need for freedom created a lack of structure, which led to this chronic absence of accountability. My team was behind me in my tailwind, simply trying to keep up to my unpredictable flight patterns. I recognize that I can't change who I am—and I don't really want to. What I *can* do is put systems in place and then get out of the way. Maybe structure would create safety and predictability that would allow my freedom and flexibility in a comfortable—but not frantic—way.

> As the father figure in this family, I was part of the problem.

Since I no longer wanted to be commander and chief, we needed to create something entirely new. Less of the inconsistent me and more involvement from the team. Leaderless. I began by exploring different technologies that might offer an organized way to track tasks and deadlines. My hope was that the technology would send automatic emails reminding my team of pending deadlines and alerting them of overdue tasks (ideally with a loud alarm, flashing lights and fireworks, but that may be too much to ask). I could potentially appoint one or two staff members to monitor and coordinate the system—like a scrum master does in agile software development environments. By implementing this form of systemized accountability, I could stand back, monitor, and let the technology do the work.

The one caveat to this systemized plan is that it would require disciplined participation from the team. They would actually need to use and respond to the technology in order for this to work. If they chose to ignore their reminders, or if they did not record their tasks, the entire system would crumble. I didn't want to remind them—or worse, force them—to participate. That was the equivalent of not using the system at all, of me continuing to act as the father figure, the disciplinarian. So the question became, how could I get my team to buy into the system we chose?

My initial thought was that it might be helpful for my team to choose the program we decided to use. They were, afterall, the ones who would need to buy into its usefulness.

I needed to involve them in the process and the first step was to facilitate a brainstorming session. What will help you do your job better? Where can technology help us be more effective? Where are our inefficiencies? How can we distribute the decision-making process so that not everything is dependent on me?

We elected a leader who researched various technologies and presented options to the group. In this scenario, I was not the one telling them what to do, but I was the facilitator, the guide. They came up with the ideas. They did the groundwork. My role was to share my observation—that we may wish to consider options for accountability—and then I needed to step back and let my team take over. My hope was that if the decision-making process was driven by my team, the likelihood of them consistently using the tool would increase.

In an attempt to create motivation and incorporate a bit of fun, we decided to offer incentives for using the new system. Together, we decided on micro finish lines that would offer rewards upon completion. I wanted my team to go beyond just *using* the technology. My hope was that they would love the efficiency it offered and get ahead of schedule, beating deadlines. A little competition might inspire my team, so we decided to make it a game.

GAMIFICATION

My team is mainly composed of individuals who fall into Generation Z. Most of them are in their mid- to late-twenties and for many, this is their first job. They're in the first season of their careers. I had a feeling they would respond well to short bursts of fun and games. I needed to match their attention spans with an activity and gamify tasks that needed to be done. This seemed to be the right approach. The key to this being successful was creating friendly competition amongst teams and the teams needed to create the rules.

Each team could create its own culture and identity—however, those decisions would need to reflect Student Village values. The teams would then compete with each other in various ways. I periodically offered incentives for the team who made the most progress. Teammates would take on challenges together, encourage each other to push through stressful times, and stay focused. I was hopeful this approach would increase motivation and productivity.

When pitching this to my team, I needed to be clear that the game belonged to them, not to me. I would ask them to draft the rules, the vision, the finish lines and the rewards. Although the final approval would be given by me, the game would be designed and agreed upon by them.

While I would have liked to be present during these initial planning sessions, I recognized the importance of keeping my mouth shut. It would no longer be my job to drive the conversation. I didn't want to sway decision-making, or impose my authority over the staff. It would be hard, but if I truly wished to become a facilitator and to offer leadership roles to my employees, I needed to show them my trust and faith.

CHAPTER SEVENTEEN
AFTER THE CHANGE

I decided to invite my team to come together on a Sunday morning—with the intention of reorganizing Student Village in a way that served us all in a more inspiring and efficient manner. I wanted to dismantle our structure and co-create an organization that we could all thrive in. My team was equally excited and anxious—but perhaps not entirely trusting of my ability to not only loosen the reins, but to let go of them entirely. Not all of them could envision Student Village in this way, without a commander and chief.

I knew this meeting would be difficult for me—to walk into this event with no agenda, opinion, or ego—so I chose to hire a facilitator to guide and ground us, thereby removing all perceived authority from me. In fact, there were times when I left the room entirely, so that my team could feel free to be honest and candid without fearing my reaction. This is not to say that hiring a facilitator is a must though. Being aware of my own emotional ties to the business I had built, it felt best for me to ask for help in its reorganization.

I'm sure you are hoping this chapter contains a step-by-step guide titled "How to Restructure Your Business." I'm sorry to disappoint you but that checklist-style manual simply cannot be written. So much of a company's organizational structure is contextual—the shared purpose of the company, its history, employees, and culture. It would be impossible to write a one-size-fits-all prescription. I *can* offer my own experience, as well as suggestions that may inspire your own journey.

PREPARATION

Before our team planning session, the facilitator suggested I read a brilliant book called *Brave New Work*. In it, author Aaron Dignan writes about traditional and non-traditional workflow, likening it to vehicle traffic. He explains that most inter**section**s use traffic lights to control the flow of vehicles. The installation of traffic lights assumes that drivers can't be trusted to make their own decisions, that they need to be told what to do, when to halt and when to move forward. Traffic lights remove the need for people to think, relying, instead on compliance and control.

Traffic lights metaphorically explain the traditional structure of workplace bureaucracy. Employees need to be managed within a hierarchy of authority, subjected to directives and permissions. They are not encouraged to think for themselves, only to stay in their own lane, working and proceeding as they are told.

Dignan then presents the analogy of a roundabout (or traffic circle). A roundabout implies not only that drivers can be trusted to make decisions for themselves, but that we must trust the decisions of others with whom we share the road. Roundabouts require drivers to be present and to be responsible for their own safety as well as the safety of those around them.

Interestingly, Dignan states that while roundabouts remove control and require free thinking, statistics show there are 75% less collisions and 90% less fatalities than a traffic controlled inter**section**.

Now, consider all of this in the context of your workplace. Would a roundabout workflow decrease "collisions" in the workplace? What would it increase? Productivity? Innovation? Efficiency?

GAMIFICATION

My team and I spent much of our time discussing what it might look like for them to have autonomy in choosing the projects they wanted to work on. Knowing that passion drives productivity, allowing people to find a niche within the company that inspired them seemed crucial to our success. People are much more inclined to work hard and be innovative when they feel the work they do is both interesting and important. Surprisingly, there wasn't as much reorganizing amongst teams as I had anticipated.

We then focused our conversation on enhancing the culture of teamwork and the possibility of offering group incentives rather than individual rewards. My team decided to focus on a Marvel superhero theme of gamification—something I'm not connected to, but they loved this idea wholeheartedly. While the Marvel team is made up of individual super heroes, each team member relies upon his or her own strength to make the team unbeatable. My team even tied in the concept of Marvel infinity gems from the movie, each individual team adopting one of the gems as an identifying trait—mind, power, reality, soul, space and time. Now, while these infinity gems mean nothing to me, what *did* matter was that each team was beginning to form a shared identity and purpose which encouraged them to come together as a whole.

STARTING SMALL

As the day progressed, the facilitator suggested we engage in an open and honest conversation about our current workplace culture. What was working? What was not working? One of the issues that arose was the noise level in our office. To provide some context, Student Village offers an open and collaborative workspace and because our team is young and vibrant, they value a fun and social atmosphere in the office. While it's awesome to have this bustling atmosphere, it can also be quite loud and distracting for those who need to focus.

There was often a group of people who were being noisy and didn't realize how disruptive they were, but no one wanted to say anything. Eventually someone would get fed up and complain to me, and I would become the default noise moderator, a role I resented. That was the old way of doing things. We decided to scrap that mentality and co-create a new, better solution. Together, my team agreed upon a solution that was not only effective, but innovative. They decided to create "zones" within the office. Some zones allow for animated conversation and others are dedicated to quiet, concentrated work. It was an idea I never would have thought of and it didn't require any monitoring from me. It was the best case scenario. Now, everyone became accountable for workplace noise in a way that balanced fun and respect for one another. Also, because they worked together to solve a problem that *they* deemed important, there was instant buy-in on the proposed course of action.

This was a small victory, but a meaningful one. While the issue of workplace noise may seem insignificant compared to deadlines, budget, customer satisfaction and other larger company needs, this exercise proved that a) I didn't need to be involved in the identification of, or solving of, this issue and b) my team could work collaboratively to create agreed-upon values and expectations. It was a lightbulb moment for all of us.

From there, the ease and ownership of decision-making had a ripple effect amongst the team at Student Village. As their confidence in our new organization grows, my own theory that this was the right decision at the right time was validated. We were heading in the right direction.

ADVICE

Aaron Dignan writes that it's a common misperception that people resist change. He suggests that people don't resist change itself, but "they resist incoherent efforts to change."[37] We often conceptualize grandiose ideas of transformation but fail to follow up with a tangible plan and consistent commitment to "go beyond the bureaucracy." Sustainable change is not a dramatic shift in direction, a static one-time event, but is a daily, actionable mentality. Dignan writes that people are actually very likely to support change which they believe will serve them well.

In his book, *Brave New Work*, Dignan offers a variety of strategies that may help to restructure your operating system in a way which shares authority and accountability. This is not a recipe to be followed verbatim, but more of a buffet-style list of suggestions for you to select what may serve the purpose of your company.

- Create a clear and inspirational purpose for your organization, for each team and for each individual role within the company

---

37   "Brave New Work: Are You Ready to Reinvent Your Organization?," (Aaron Dignan, February 2019), https://www. bravenewwork.com/.

- Normalize mistake-making
  - Celebrate "noble failure," encourage regular debriefs and judgment-free retrospectives— mistakes are learning opportunities!
- Ask for advice instead of permission
- Clarify decision-making rights held by teams and roles

Encourage the giving and receiving of feedback as a means for the constant pursuit of improvement

- Allow freedom for employees to choose when, where and how they work
- Eliminate processes and policies that no longer make sense
- Define spending thresholds for which employees do not need to seek approval
- Fill leadership roles through volunteerism, consensus or election
- Create transparency in roles, policies, and documents
- Offer collective, team-based rewards instead of individual rewards
- Foster a mentality that invites employees to work and think differently

Transformation does not come from dipping your toe in the water. It's a dive into the deep end of the pool. In reorganizing my own company, I wanted to tip the scales in a way that made it impossible to go back to the status quo, as it no longer served us. This required me to make a conscious decision to trust my team—which was a dramatic reframing of my previous belief structure.

Previously, as the sole leader of Student Village, I believed that the team needed to prove their worth and earn my trust. This was the source of not only my control issues, but my anxiety, as well as my profound exhaustion and frustration. I had created a system of traffic lights that relied on me to control the operation of my company's workflow. Even though my beliefs limited me, my team and my company's potential, I was too afraid to let go of control. I realized the foundational error of my thinking was that trust was to be *earned*. In dismantling the hierarchical structure of Student Village and installing a roundabout workflow, we were laying a foundation of mutual trust from which everything else will grow.

> We were laying a foundation of mutual trust from which everything else will grow.

SECTION 6:

CHANGE BEGINS WITH US

CHAPTER EIGHTEEN
REWIRING THE FUTURE

As I wrote this book, I began to see examples of decentralized systems all around me—in business and in nature—and I began to ask myself, "What can this teach us about youth and the future?"

In a recent article by Brandon Quittem called "Bitcoin is the Mycelium of Money,"[38] he makes a brilliant comparison between the cryptocurrency and the root structure of fungi. What is remarkable about the structure of mycelium is that it seems to be a decentralized communication system in which everything works together to serve the whole. Scientists call it the "'wood wide web', a system where "millions of species of fungi and bacteria swap nutrients between soil

---

38   1 "Bitcoin is The Mycelium of Money," (Brandon Quittem, May 1, 2020.) https://www.brandonquittem.com/bitcoin-is-the-mycelium-of-money/.

and the roots of trees, forming a vast, interconnected web of organisms throughout the woods."[39] Mycelium are capable of communicating, and acting as a defense mechanism, for the survival of many plants and trees—warding off harmful bacteria and sending extra nutrients to those who are threatened.

The wood wide web is an aptly named system, making direct comparisons to the world wide web—the preferred form of gathering and communicating. Like mycelium, youth are using online platforms to gather in likeminded tribes, forming a defense mechanism for survival, calling for a better, kinder world than the one they inherited.

Earlier in this book, we explored Bitcoin as a leaderless organization and Brandon Quittem takes this idea one step further. He cleverly compares Bitcoin to mycelium, both having no centralized point of control and intentionally creating systems that prevent one group or individual from manipulating the whole. Both Bitcoin and mycelium seem to be organized in a way that makes them resilient to attacks.

Quittem explains that bitcoin is "made up of individuals with their own perspectives, motivations and abilities. Collectively, they form a consensus on the rules of the game." It is a collaborative organization, based on an agreed upon code

---

39   "'Wood wide web'—the underground network of microbes that connects trees—mapped for first time," (Gabriel Popkin, May 15, 2019) https://www.sciencemag.org/news/2019/05/wood-wide-web-underground-network-microbes-connects-trees-mapped-first-time.

of conduct where the individual contributors work together toward a common goal - freedom from institutional control, otherwise known as traditional banking systems. Likewise, mycelium are made up of individual networks that share membranes, allowing them to communicate in relation to the allocation of resources, reproduction and strategies for defense against competing organisms. Quittem quotes Paul Stamets who further explains information sharing in mycelium, "which are aware, react to change and collectively have the long-term health of the host-environment in mind." To me, this sounds a lot like youth—a large portion of the world's population that have the long-term care of humanity in mind.

Like mycelium and Bitcoin, young people are using a structure of communication to expand and adapt. They are using tools of connection to create strong, scalable intentions. As support for their hopes and values grow, they are becoming a force to be reckoned with. When we look at mycelium and Bitcoin, we can see that decentralized networks—when they have reached their critical mass—are incredibly influential. The point of breach has arrived.

Generation Z was born into a world of exponential disruptions—in the realms of politics, finance, environment, equality, and consciousness—and in this world of disruption, we are all struggling to find meaning. The world as we know it is laden with polarity, segregation, antiquated ideas and outdated systems. In order to move past this, we need to let go of what is no longer serving us and create a planet made up of strong ethics. Gen Z craves just that. They want to rewrite the world so that it is kinder and cleaner. They want a world based in fairness and equality. They desire flexibility, connection and a life of passion and purpose.

This generation was born and raised with a different set of factory settings than you or I. They connect differently. They learn differently. They think differently. They have a different world view. We may not fully understand Gen Z yet, but what if understanding them became our primary goal? Imagine how we could change our current reality if we chose to find points of connection instead of resisting what we don't understand. Imagine the possibilities if we chose to support and nurture those differences instead of asking youth to conform. Imagine the impact we could make if young people and elders worked together instead of in opposition.

This is not to say that all young people share these noble goals. As with everything, there are two ends to the spectrum. In fungi, we have mycelium but we also have parasitic fungi which cause plant disease. With Bitcoin, there are the masses who have embraced decentralization and there are also those who choose to manipulate the cryptocurrency by buying and selling huge amounts of it in the sport market in an attempt to impact the price. Youth also fall on a spectrum.

Author Jamie Wheal refers to the book ends of this spectrum as fundamentalists and nihilists. He explains that as religion takes a less significant role in society, we are experiencing a collective collapse of meaning. Fundamentalists try to restore meaning by clinging to their faith, thinking their beliefs are the *only* truth. Nihilists, on the other hand, respond by claiming that life has no meaning or purpose at all. If we remain on the ends of the spectrum—grasping to make sense of a nonsensical world—progress is slow or nonexistent. To make change we must meet in the middle.

Wheal goes on to ask how we can make meaning for everyone instead of only for a select few. He suggests that in moments of chaos (society as we know it), we need to become more rooted to those around us. Connection is the key. We need to work collectively to decide on our story, our goals and how we commit to working toward them together.

My point is that the future has yet to be written. We get to decide. We can journey down one road and create a more sustainable planet. If we capitulate to the other side, we will find a more intense version of what we have today. We don't know how this will end. My guess is that there will be many breaches along the way—some good and some traumatic. Our best chance at success comes in the form of elders and youth collaborating. There's no promise that youth will push us to the other side, toward a better future. They have fundamentalists and nihilists, just as we do. We can hope they will organize themselves and work toward change, but it is not a given. They can't do it on their own. We need to do this as a collective.

According to Jamie Wheal, the guardrails that used to define our existence—religion, family structure, corporate hierarchy—are facing a relevance crisis in today's world. I think the elders are the new guardrails. We should keep young people on their path toward their brilliance. We should harness their energy, and their progress toward change but in order to do this effectively, we need to let go of some of our outdated beliefs.

Let's think about all of this and what it might mean for your business, for your brand. Companies are simply a microcosm of what is happening in the larger world. Just like there are disconnects and limits in the world, you will also find these challenges in your organization. Most likely, it is not just a manager and employee disconnect, but one based on values. When fault lines appear, it is a warning to leadership, a heads up. The world is not just changing *out there*. It needs to change *in here* too. You need to walk the walk when it comes to your values. If you don't, there will be friction, tension, rampant employee activism and a cancel culture within your company.

In your business and in the world, there has never been a more perfect time to find meaning, to do things differently, and to help our younger generations develop the tools they need to change the course of the world. We need to understand that the relationship between elders and youth is symbiotic. We can learn as much from them as they can from us. We also need to hold multiple perspectives and diverse points of view. Having an attitude of *and,* not *or* is what creates the possibility of a different outcome.

My greatest hope is that we can draw inspiration from each other. Young people are the key to a better future and we can help them get there by getting out of the way. We need to drop our resistance and ask how we can nurture their critical thinking. We shape them with our wisdom and at the same time, we need to be open to the lessons *we* need to learn about how to help fix the world we have created.

Perhaps the irony of this book—the punchline of it all—is that, as I go through my life, I don't see young and old. I don't see generations. I see people. I see people who are at different levels of knowledge, experience, wisdom and consciousness. You can meet a switched on, conscious sixteen-year-old and you can meet an uninformed, unconscious sixty-year-old. Time gives you an opportunity to raise your game and your awareness, but it is not a guarantee. Not all elders are wise. Not all youth are naive. Old and young, elders and youth, wise and naive—we are all in it together.

My personal goal is to continue connecting youth and elders. In the ever-changing chaotic world, a decentralized, leaderless approach seems to be the best way to be agile and adapt. In the future, I plan to continue my work with elders, helping them make sense of themselves and this new world we find ourselves in.

> Old and young, elders and youth, wise and naive—we are all in it together.

If I've done my job well, you should be feeling hopeful. I also want to leave you with a word of caution. When we are all learning together, and when we hold multiple perspectives, it isn't always easy. Breach isn't pretty and her expression isn't incremental. It's an explosion of disruptive possibility that will hopefully bring us closer to the world we want as opposed to the world we have.

As this book comes to a close, I find myself thinking about the word *breach* once again. What if the breach is only the first step?

We tend to focus our attention on the destructive nature of the breach but I suggest you think of it like a forest fire— devastating but followed by regenerative growth. We need to accept the breach for what it is and shift our focus to the possibilities that come on the other side of it - the opportunity to recalibrate the world, collectively.

What if breaching is not a destruction of what we know, but an opportunity to reorient the world with a higher purpose? What if breaching isn't about coming apart, but is about coming back together? After the breach comes a coalescing which forges stronger bonds—between families, companies and communities—than ever before.

Breach—a painful process, beautiful in its brutality, and necessary for forward evolution.

When a single person takes a stand, this energy ignites the manifestation process and sparks the possibility of change. In this book, we have taken a look at an entire generation which has collectively taken a stand. Young people have individually and simultaneously stood up and decided to fight, wanting to make the world a better place. This interconnectedness (much like a mycelium network) has created something big enough to manifest global change.

The time has come for the elders to get out of the way and make room for Gen Z to step into their full potential so that we may all reap the benefits of their hopes and dreams.

ABOUT THE AUTHOR

A man of many talents—youth marketing expert, active trail junkie, dynamic public speaker and thought-provoking author—Ronen Aires is passionate about a lot of things after a good cup of coffee. As the renowned co-founder and CEO of Student Village, South Africa's most prominent student marketing and graduate development specialists, Ronen dedicated much of his career to supporting youth and guiding them towards greatness. Whether its speaking on podcasts and news programs, or writing articles and a book, Ronen utilizes all available platforms to highlight the genius of today's young adults.

In his roles as global activist and investor, Ronen excitedly shares his knowledge of psychedelic healing and breathwork. He strongly advocates for the importance of living a full and holistic lifestyle, encouraging others to accelerate their potential by embracing ancient wisdom.

Ronen Aires is a husband, father, advocate, entrepreneur, guide, and investor among many other things. His preferred title? Young Elder.